FEEDBACK LOOP
Designing Complex Architecture

Kyle Talbott

Kyle William Talbott Publisher
PO Box 070435
Milwaukee WI 53207 USA
Telephone 414 483 1460
ktalbott@uwm.edu

ISBN 978-0-615-34982-4

CONTENTS

INTRODUCTION

Feedback Loop introduces contemporary experimental architecture. It identifies key concepts underlying the work of leading experimenters in the field. It distinguishes emerging ideas from those of past generations, and it predicts a future for the work that might become a reality, if this fledgling movement continues to take root and grow.

To clarify the methods and goals of a movement in its formative stage requires a willingness to interpret ideas not yet solidified. This makes *Feedback Loop* a manifesto as well as a summary. It seeks not only to describe current momentum in the field, but to push it in an optimistic direction.

The recent literature offers many manifestos, but they are often technologically-focused and jargon-filled. The intended audience seems to be other experimenters who are already familiar with the ideas and committed to the cause. This can make it difficult for novices to find an entry point into contemporary thought, which serves only to arrest growth of the movement. *Feedback Loop* cuts through the jargon and presents key ideas in plain language, and in doing so, it depolarizes avant-garde and mainstream. If the new movement is to succeed, its ideas must become more accessible.

Feedback Loop assumes no prior knowledge of the subject, but some knowledge of design is helpful. To ease readers into the subject, early chapters establish a context for discussion and define key concepts. Later chapters then revisit the concepts, seeing them as components in a larger system of thought that gives a cohesive identity to the new movement.

As the identity of a movement solidifies, efforts are made to coin a name. Many have circulated in the literature, but none have yet won a definitive following. Names such as Biomimicry and Biomorphism focus too narrowly on the renewed interest in Nature as a source of inspiration, without identifying the motivation for such an interest. Another is Parametricism, which focuses too narrowly on a design method rather than a goal. The name Morphogenetic Architecture seems too enigmatic to endure, but it does identify a deeper interest of the movement: microscopic constituents of things as driver of their macroscopic nature. In lieu of coining a name, *Feedback Loop* refers to the fledgling movement simply as *complex architecture*. The concept of complexity might be too broad of an umbrella, but I prefer to err on the side of under-constricting the territory. I will also refer to it even more innocuously as the *new movement*.

Designers are flooded with images of complex buildings and discussion of sophisticated digital technology, but not much is said about the *how* and the *why* of complex architecture. Designing complex architecture involves far more than learning how to write scripts and use a waterjet cutter. Even less is said about *why* designers might want complexity. *Feedback Loop* answers these questions. It digs beneath the surface and looks for substantive methods and reasons, and it offers tangible advice about how to engage the creative challenges and opportunities, which lie beyond form-making and digital stunts. *Feedback Loop* is an antidote for anyone caught up in the pursuit of complexity as a fashion statement or as a technological game. It describes why we need complex architecture, and why its motives, methods and tools are crucial to the future of the discipline.

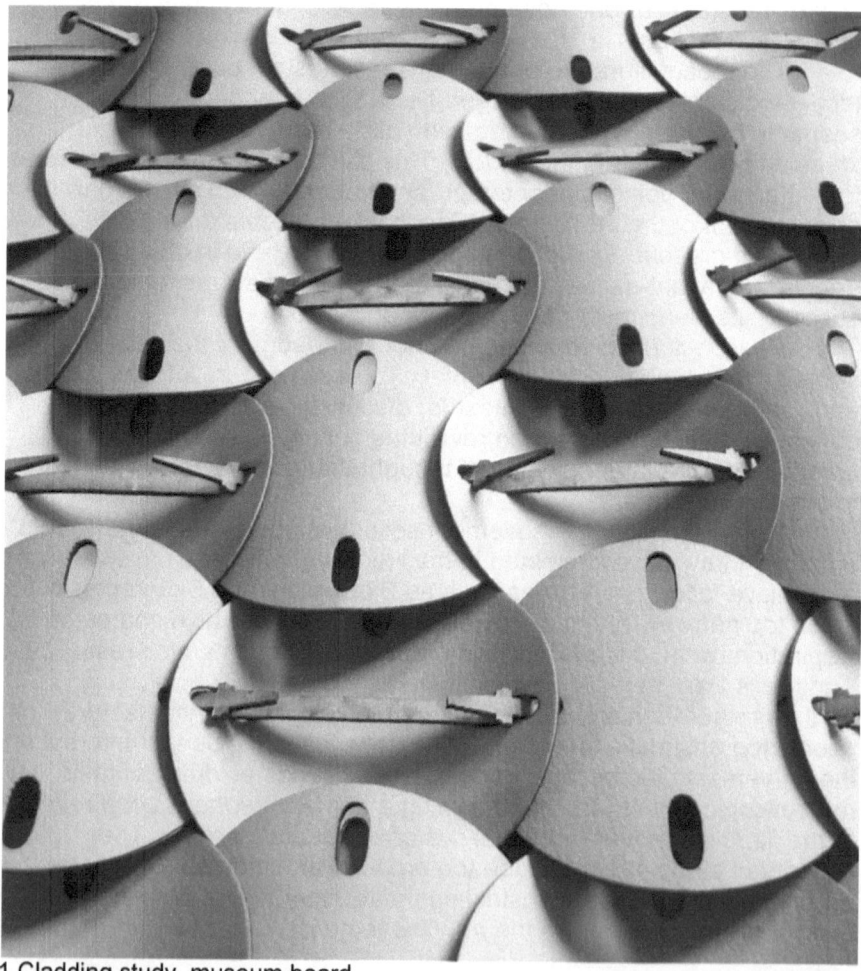

1 Cladding study, museum board

Feedback Loop

EXPERIMENTATION

To pursue complex architecture designers must relinquish conventional practice. Rather than live by the rote procedures of the mainstream, they must embrace a process of testing and discovery. This process of experimentation relies on a collection of underlying concepts: innovation, creativity, inspiration, conviction, integrity and vision, which define its nature and establish a context for the discussion of complex architecture. These are the core virtues of the experimental designer, which lay a foundation for the pursuit of complexity. They underlie most discussion of complex architecture, but they are rarely acknowledged. They are unspoken aspects of design, which designers tend to take for granted, yet are indispensible to any process of experimentation. This chapter acknowledges them and offers suggestions about how to adopt them.

Innovation

An *innovation* is something new and better than what existed before. Innovations can be small, like the Post-It, which merely takes a traditional notepad and adds a strip of adhesive along one edge. Or an innovation can be big, like Copernicus' explanation of the movement of planets. Regardless of size, innovations open new possibilities by extending knowledge or enhancing action. This is why innovations are the most valuable commodity. Every ambitious professional, business and industry hunts for them. Sometimes the leaders of a business convince themselves otherwise: that it is wise to maintain a steady state, but the steady state is a myth. Sooner or later such businesses wane.

The central value a designer offers is the creation of something better than what a client or customer already has. In architecture, clients who simply want "more of the same" do not benefit from design. They would do better to hire a real estate developer, who specializes in the efficient production of established solutions. Just by walking through the door of a design firm, clients imply a desire for something new and better. It is true that architects also provide other services, such as construction document production, but these follow after and depend on the invention of new and better designs.

Notice that even in support services, architects want innovation. In the past decade, the broken process of construction documentation was widely lamented. Those who figure out a better way to document a project for construction gain a valuable competitive advantage.

Despite the value of innovation, it is often disparaged. Sometime innovators are accused of chasing after fashion, unconcerned with cultural values established over centuries. But innovators are deeply concerned with history. Since an innovation is better than what came before, it can only be evaluated in reference to what came before. Innovators do not ignore history; they learn from it and transcend it.

Sometimes innovation is pitted against mastery. By embracing new technologies and methods, innovators render obsolete established expertise. Expertise in the piloting of dirigibles was devalued by the invention of the airplane. Expertise in load-bearing masonry construction was devalued by the invention of modern reinforced concrete. Just as designers begin to master something, a variant emerges, which requires them to shelve their mastery and relearn. This seems to erode mastery, since it requires a lifetime of diligent practice. When the innovator suggests to the master that his methods, lovingly studied for decades, are now obsolete, the master's accomplishment is devalued. When the master argues that more is gained from intense study of established methods, the innovator's accomplishment is likewise devalued.

This polarity is an illusion. Without mastery, the full potential of new methods and products cannot be realized, since they require refinement over time. Without innovation, mastery loses purpose, hardening over time into rote formula. Innovation and mastery are complementary processes, each essential to human progress.

Creativity

Creativity is the thought process that brings innovations into existence. While mainstream practice tends to segregate activities as creative or non-creative, experimental practice desegregates. Budgets are not obstructions but resources that buy opportunities. Deadlines are not constrictions but tools for orchestrating collaborative work. Fabrication is not a nuisance that gets in the way of form-making, but a catalyst for exploration. In mainstream practice those who manage budgets, schedules and construction are often treated as non-creative, which attempts to absolve them from participating in design, but this segregation is an illusion conjured by the non-creative. It is an attempt to make a sanctuary where they can escape the imperative to innovate.

Conventional segregation is fueled by popular myths about the nature of creativity. Most laypersons and many architects believe it is a gift possessed by a lucky few, which endows them with an ability to generate something new and better out of thin air. To the contrary, creativity is a tangible skill, one that is different from learning how to type a letter or draw a gutter detail, but a skill nonetheless. *Creativity* is the ability to bring a new and better alternative into existence by means of a non-obvious recombination.

An alternative is creative only if it is *non-obvious*. An alternative is not creative if it is already established or reached automatically by following established rules. Creativity is the non-routine, the non-automated. If you write a random 100-digit number on a piece of paper, chances are, you are the first person ever to write it. However, doing so is a rote act of number writing. It is not enough to make something new; creativity makes something new that is not easy to see or to find. It involves a process of exploration and discovery.

An alternative is creative only if it is a *recombination* of existing knowledge. Nothing can be created in a vacuum. Designers use their past experiences as building-blocks for the new. Creativity is a process of recombining past experience in new ways to form new products. The constituent elements are not new, only the way they combine. The essence of creativity is integration: the putting together of known ingredients in previously unknown ways.

Generating recombinations is an unpredictable process. Sometimes it breeds innovation, sometimes it regurgitates known combinations. In order to complete the creative process, the act of recombination must continue iteratively until something new and better emerges. An important aspect of creativity, then, is a choice to discard the first answers that come to mind, and search for more answers until something new and better is found. This means that creativity is part skill and part attitude. The skill needs to be honed, but what differentiates creative from non-creative persons is also desire. A person has to *want* to be creative. He has to *want* to find the new and better, and to persist in his search until he does.

Inspiration

Designers often note that anything around them might spark an idea. The mind can find anywhere the material it needs for non-obvious recombinations. This is inspiration. The search for inspiration is the search for situations fertile with the potential to spark creative ideas. It involves immersing oneself in a situation: an environment or material or technique or technology or imagery, so that one becomes fully receptive to the possibilities it holds.

Inspiration is the groundwork designers do leading up to the creative act. Inspiration is the experiential nutrients designers feed their minds, the things they observe, the places they go, the ideas they study, the methods they employ, which increases the mind's readiness to create. Inspiration supplements the material recorded in memory with provocative fresh material. Together memory and inspiration fuel

Experimentation

creative recombination. For example, a designer might combine childhood memories of camping trips in the mountains with imagery from classic monster movies to create an ominous, secluded residence in the woods.

Designers need diverse and potent sources of inspiration, which they can tap without waiting for others to take the lead. Those who wait for others to hand them creative ideas are not rewarded in practice. Experimental designers are creatively independent, and they become so by building an arsenal of sources of inspiration, which they tap whenever they need ideas.

Feedback Loop discusses sources of inspiration important in recent experimental work, but some designers struggle to tap them. Some designers believe that inspiration is indefensible. Instead, they seek quantifiable, scientific-sounding explanations for their design decisions. Designers exposed to this kind of pressure might become averse to creativity. They might stop looking for inspiration. Another obstacle is habit. When designers coast along in their comfort-zone, they lose a frame of mind conducive to inspiration. They look right past it.

Conviction

A *conviction* is a belief about some fundamental aspect of life or the world. Convictions transcend the trivial aspects of daily life and instead establish a position with regard to larger, over-arching concerns. One does not hold a conviction about one's favorite brand of fruit spread, but one might hold a conviction about the role of nutrition in life.

A conviction is a belief accepted and lived-by with passion. People cherish them, nurture them, and fight for them in the face of opposition. One might be indifferent about which restaurant to visit for dinner, given a few healthy options, but if one has a conviction to live a full and healthy life by eating a well-balanced diet, then one will resist the option to binge on fried potatoes and milk shakes.

Once it is formed, a conviction endures. Convictions are not like personal preferences, which come and go with time and fashion. A conviction is a long-term commitment, something seen as important to life in the long run. If one has a conviction about good nutrition, then one still might binge on fried potatoes and milk shakes in a moment of weakness, but if this happens, one does not feel good about it later. Acting against one's convictions detours life down an undesirable path. The detour might be small or large depending on the circumstances, but it is a detour nonetheless.

While it is possible to change a conviction, this usually happens only after close consideration of a lot of evidence and arguments, which eventually become persuasive. For example, if a person believes it is healthy to eat a balanced diet, it would be difficult to convince him that everything he knows about green vegetables is wrong, and it is actually binging on fried potatoes and milk shakes that will best protect his long-term health.

When a person bundles together a collection of convictions, which together identify a point of view regarding many aspects of life, they form a view of the world. A *view of the world* is a comprehensive perspective on what is important about the world and life in it. It is a person's convictions knitted together into a consistent whole. In a view of the world, each conviction supports and strengthens the others.

It does not matter whether a person acknowledges that he has one or not, a view of the world is inevitable. A person cannot believe all things to be true, hold all goals, and live every possible life. He must choose. He chooses what to believe and what not to believe, which goals to pursue and which not to pursue, and thus his life unfolds in a particular way. Every choice he makes implies a judgment about what is more important in life and what is less important, and in this way he forms an implicit view of the world. Even if he never explicitly states it or acknowledges it, it is there. By choosing one alternative course of action over others, he implies that all the expected events, consequences and rewards that lie along that course are preferable to the other courses open to him [1].

A view of the world is also implied by the choices he makes in design. When a designer creates a building, he chooses one design among millions. The fact that he chooses it over all the rest implies that it is somehow more suitable. This is true down to every detail he chooses to include. A building, because its creation is an act of choice, always involves an evaluation of what is *better* and *worse*, more *conducive* to human life and more *corrosive*. It always expresses some aspect of a designer's view of the world.

There is no escaping it. Even if a designer makes choices by flipping a coin (or other random process), the resulting building still expresses his view of the world. In this case it expresses a world in which human purpose is futile, in which mankind's relationship to Nature is uncontrollable, and in which we are adrift in chaos. This is the wider implication of choosing to make everything in life, or in a building, random.

At this point some designers might ask: If our choices inevitably imply a set of convictions, and if these convictions, knitted together as a view of the world, inevitably get expressed in architecture, then why be concerned with convictions? It seems like they just take care of themselves.

While convictions are fundamental to life and formed even unknowingly, convictions are not best formed this way. Doing so leaves designers vulnerable to the worst sort of ideas, adopted

Experimentation

uncritically from a mish-mash of dubious sources: mainstream news media, pop psychology, the entertainment industry and popular opinion. Even though some semblance of a view of the world is inevitable, the successful integration of convictions into a *coherent* view of the world is not. Furthermore, a view of the world is not automatically integrated coherently in architecture. Coherence requires discipline and self-reflection.

Designers who leave their convictions implicit usually make confused, diluted, sometimes even self-contradictory architecture, architecture that fights against itself. Instead of expressing a view of the world creatively and intensely, such bewildered designers stumble through the process and end up with something that is still meaningful, but in a way that is barely discernable and eminently forgettable.

To identify your convictions and their relationship to architecture, it is helpful to answer such questions as: What drives you to design? What do you want to accomplish in your work? What do you believe is important about life and the world, and how does this influence your designs? What should architecture contribute to human life? How can you define design goals in a larger context, which transcends any particular site, program or client? How can you define a vision for your design work that drives your creative thinking into the foreseeable future and brings a larger coherence and purpose to your work?

Answers to such questions, though difficult, are essential to experimental design. Experimentation requires deviation from known answers established in reference to tradition or convention. Untethered from established ideas, and without clear and forceful convictions, a designer drifts. Convictions are self-defined guideposts, chosen with independent judgment, which replace established ideas gleaned uncritically from others.

Integrity

Integrity is devotion to one's convictions, even in the face of opposition or disapproval. Identifying one's convictions is only half the battle; the other half is commitment to them in action.

We live in a confrontation-adverse society. Some designers work so hard to agree with others that they lose a sense of self. Their convictions can become so defined by what others think that there is nothing too firm within them. Their actions, consequently, take them here and then there, this way then that, reacting to what others do, rather than being straight and true, flying always toward some constant, far-off destination, toward which they navigate according to an inner compass, some conviction they hold absolutely, regardless of what others think. For designers with integrity, disagreement is not a source of anxiety. It is one way to reveal and enjoy what makes them unique.

Feedback Loop

Experimental designers have no obligation to accept the avant-garde's agenda, but because it is the day's agenda, if designers want their work to be seen as relevant, they must understand the relationship between the two. Designers who choose a different path should be able to explain why they have done so, and make a compelling argument for why their path is relevant.

Vision

Vision, like creativity and inspiration, is often misunderstood. It is thought of as the ability to see completed designs in the imagination instantaneously, the ability to magically know what to do in difficult circumstances, or the ability to predict the future. A person with vision seems to have special insight implanted by means of mystical revelation. This is not the sort of vision designers need.

Vision is what results when designers internalize the preceding virtues. *Vision* is the ability to see naturally and easily innovative designs that embody one's convictions. Vision is a kind of certainty, the certainty in one's ability to design anything and imbue it with a desired meaning. It is the certainty that one's work is a profound reflection of oneself, and that each thing one designs is contributing to a larger sum: a body of work with a worthy purpose.

When designers possess vision, the connections between their sources of inspiration, their convictions and their designs become clear. Vision is the payoff for acquiring the other virtues.

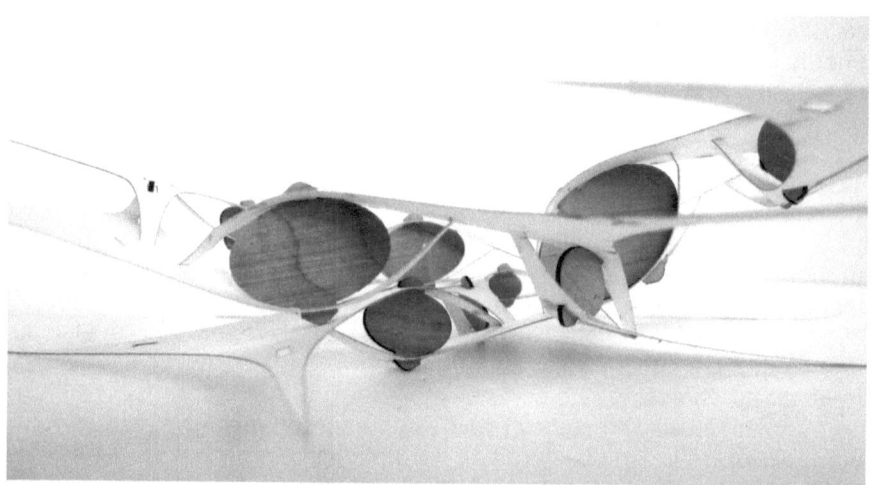

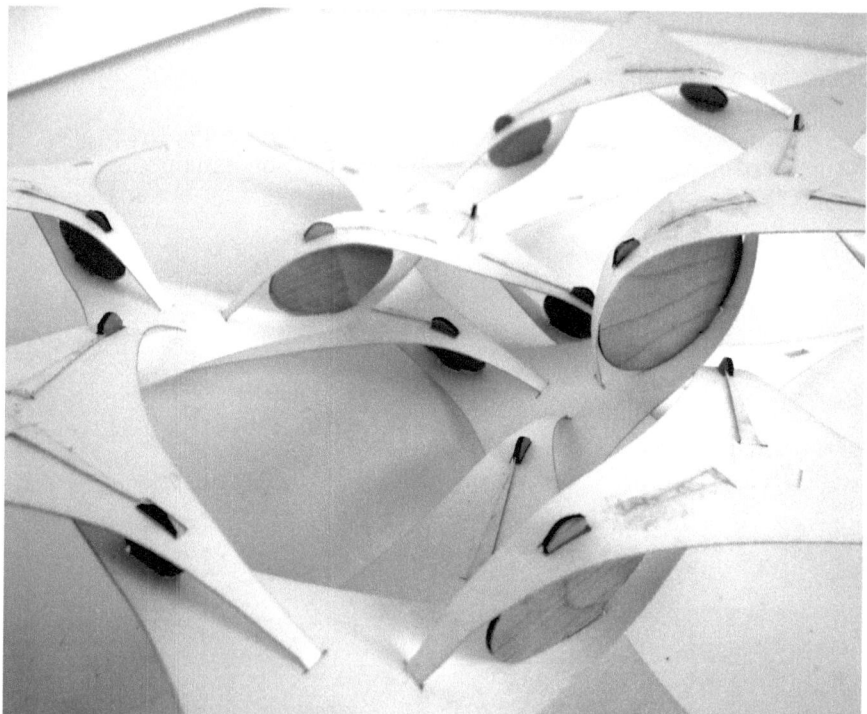

2 Structural study, paper, wood

Feedback Loop

INSIGHT THROUGH PROTOTYPING

Complex architecture resists a formalistic path, in which a formal concept comes first, and then material production follows. Instead it recognizes that a material medium provides formative inspiration. Experimental designers often search for creative insight in the properties and behaviors of materials.

An *insight* is a creative idea in raw form, before it is evaluated or refined. An insight might be good or bad, innovative or insignificant, but before it can be evaluated as such, it must erupt into awareness. Moments of insight are pivotal events in the process of creative thinking. Designers seek to traverse these mental steps: 1) a source of inspiration is used to evoke … 2) a non-obvious recombination … 3) which comes into awareness as an idea (i.e., an insight), which is then … 4) evaluated in reference to convictions … and 5) determined to be innovative or not. Insights are not only needed at the outset of a project. They are necessary at every level of development from concept to detail. Even to develop a new gutter detail, one or more insights are needed.

Great thinkers share a similar description of the moment of insight. From Galileo peering through a telescope at the moons of Jupiter to Leonardo da Vinci's observation of clouds and stains, insight results from external conditions providing the right ingredients at the right time to reveal a new possibility. For designers, external stimuli can come from their medium: the drawing and model-building materials they use or the materials of full-scale construction, which are used to make prototypes.

Prototyping is the process of making full-scale or near full-scale test versions of a design, in order to see how materials behave, and to allow those behaviors to suggest new possibilities. Building a prototype is an act of tectonic and geometric exploration in which designers focus on their interaction with a material. Through a close awareness of its potentials and limitations, designers "listen to" a material, allowing it to guide them toward new possibilities. In contrast, when designers attempt to unilaterally impose their pre-conceived goals on a material, they inevitably fight with it. Materials are finite; they cannot do everything, so designers who try to impose ideas on material usually get stuck in a creative malaise.

Experimental designers work from the premise that materials "talk back"; design becomes a process of negotiating with a material. When designers attempt to alter a material in a certain way, it resists. So they adjust their approach. By seeking out the inclinations of a material, designers discover unanticipated behaviors and adjust their goals to take advantage of them. This feedback loop turns experimental design into an act of exploring a medium, rather than executing a pre-conceived idea.

When designers explore a material, they dissect its complexity, probing below its obvious properties, standard applications and everyday forms. The value of negotiation is not only improved constructability, but discovery of hidden potential. Designers accomplish this by identifying a latent property. A *latent property* is non-obvious, present in a material by nature but suppressed by standard applications. By identifying such a property, designers identify a path to innovation.

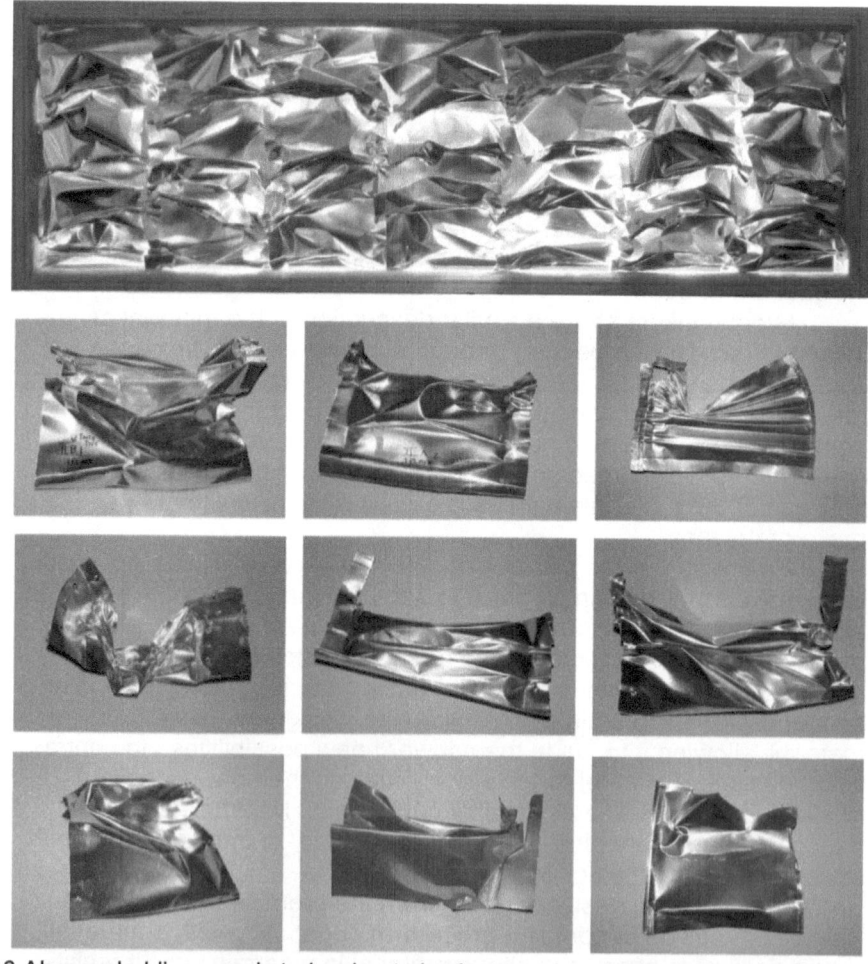

3 Above: cladding panel study, sheet aluminum and wood; Below: prototypes of crushed aluminum "scales"

Feedback Loop

Argument for a Dialogue with Materials

Part 1:

1. Every material has a finite set of properties that make up its nature.
2. This finite nature allows it to do some things, and not others. Every material is limited.
3. Designers manipulate materials (altering their size, shape and composition) in order to bring about an intentional state.
4. But designers' limited knowledge of materials can sometimes introduce a conflict: They expect a material to do something against its nature, and consequently, their intentions are thwarted.
5. *To avoid this, designers must adjust their intentions to align with what can be implemented in available materials. They must learn to recognize a material's limitations and potentials.*

Part 2:

1. For designers, the study of a material's potential does not happen in the impersonal way conducted by scientists, who test materials at a distance under neutral conditions.
2. Instead, designers explore what a material can do while designing.
3. Insights gained in this way lead to incremental adjustments of designers' intentions.
4. *Through this give-and-take interaction, designers discover new intentions and how to best implement them.*

Part 3:

1. A material possesses some properties that are obvious to the casual observer. For instance, a plank of wood is hard and heavy.
2. But a material also possesses properties that are non-obvious: things that it can do or become that require careful study to discover. These are a material's *latent* properties. A latent property of a plank of wood is its absorptivity. More latent is its ability to swell when wet. Even more latent is the visual effect of its grain as it deforms when swollen.
3. *A primary route to creative insight is the discovery and exploitation of latent properties. By accentuating a latent property, even a common material can be transformed into something new, exotic, and valuable.*

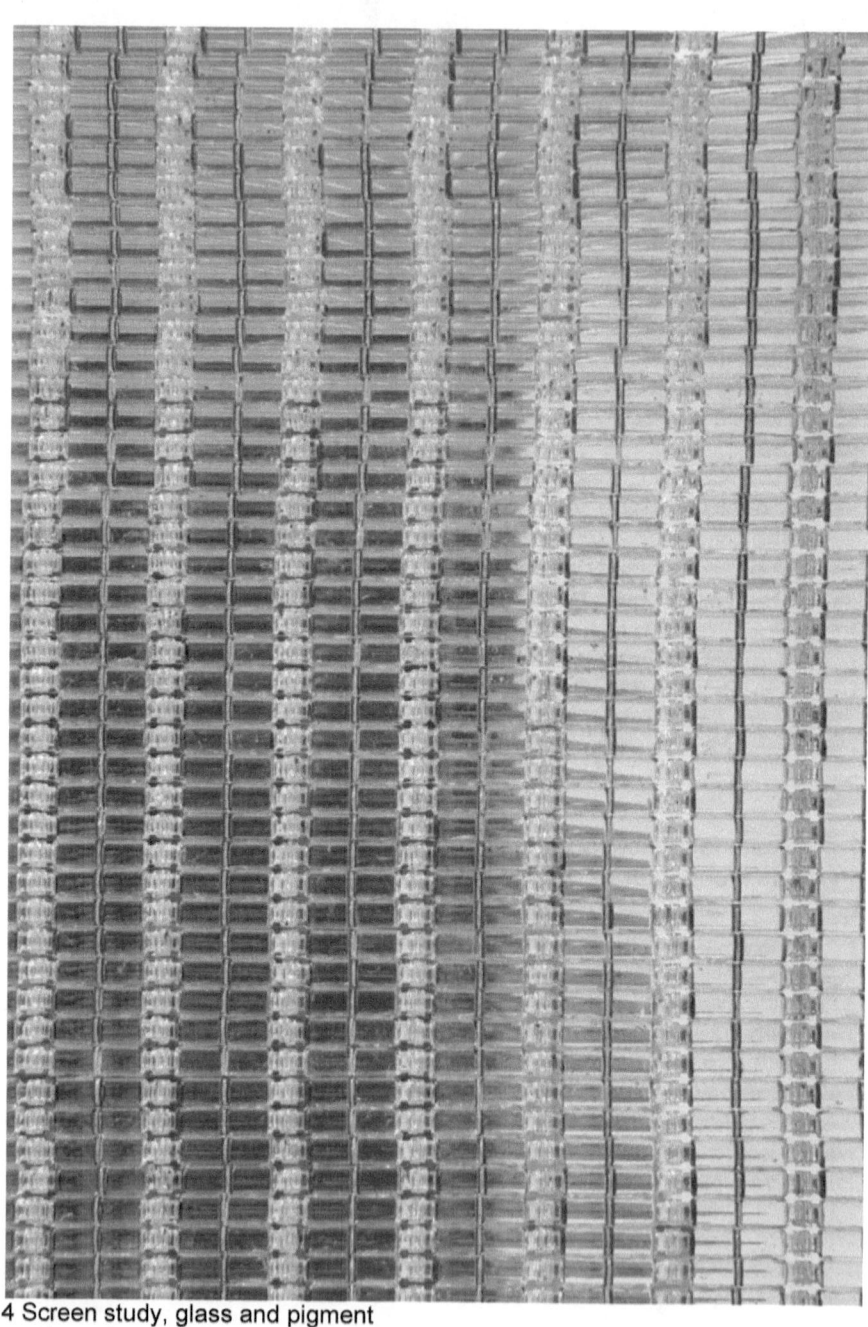

4 Screen study, glass and pigment

Feedback Loop

MOVING BETWEEN MODEL AND PROTOTYPE

A medium of visualization can be used as a crutch to avoid dealing with material reality. This is true for media from digital model-building to pencil sketching. A medium of visualization is a stand-in, which allows designers to see the reality of their designs without the time and money needed to construct them. When designers make a cardboard model or generate a digital model with a script, they selectively depict some aspects of a design for the purpose of study, while simultaneously filtering out other aspects such as its actual size and materials.

Because of this partial tethering of depiction to reality, media of visualization allow designers to forget that a depiction of a thing is not the thing. Designers can suffer the delusion that they are completing a design merely by completing a digital model, or by refining a sketch into a measured drawing, or by resolving a paper representation of a structure.

The only way to avoid this delusion is to frequently test designs at *full-scale* by constructing material prototypes. Designers need a feedback loop between a medium of visualization and the ultimate medium of the produced thing. They do not need to construct the entire building over and over again. Executing strategic fragments of the whole is usually sufficient.

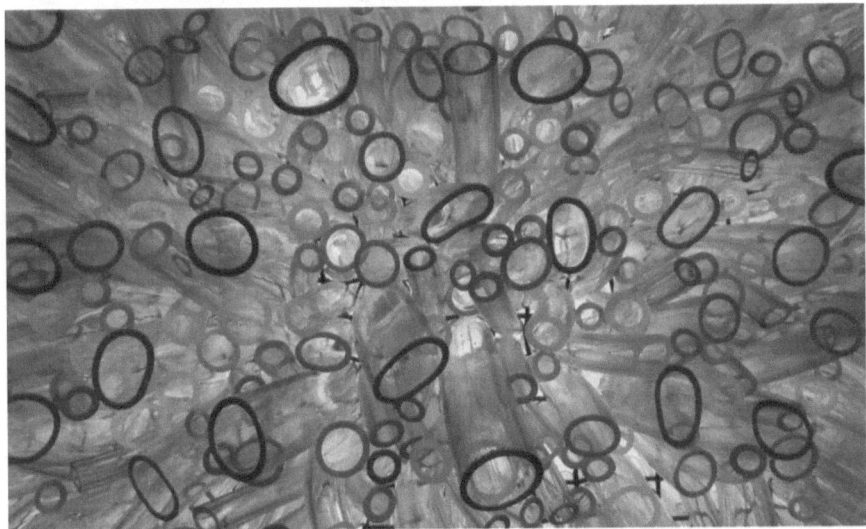

5 Close up view of a screen study, plastic tubing and wire mesh

EMBRACING THE QUALITATIVE

Design does not lead exclusively to quantifiable results: x square feet of space, x distance to another space, x amount of privacy, x number of lumens. In the act of making, designers shape a qualitative world. They distribute square feet of space with a degree of containment or openness, they position adjacent spaces with a degree of intimacy, they create subtle gradients of privacy, and they distribute lumens across a surface in an endless variety of patterns.

By accentuating certain qualities, architecture shapes a setting for a certain kind of life. It submerges the events of daily life in an atmosphere that accentuates a relentless struggle for career success, or relinquishment of grand dreams in favor of simple pleasures. It accentuates a bond with family, or it intensifies consuming work. In the atmospheres we inhabit, we experience a heightened state of tranquility or conflict, confusion or clarity. We find traces of what is sacred, of what is the proper focus of life.

The qualities of a building, its luminosity and gradients, its textures and edges, its articulation and shape, its thickness and transparency, its encapsulations and continuities, are what take an environment beyond minimum functional requirements to manifest important qualities of life or the world.

Digital media present a challenge to qualitative design. Because these media are essentially quantitative, their developers struggle to capture and manage qualitative information. Although they are slowly getting better, digital visualization remains thin on qualities. The strength of digital media is the representation and manipulation of abstract geometry. In the foreseeable future, to engage the full, rich spectrum of the world's qualities, designers must engage the stuff of the world: a material medium.

Making material prototypes heightens awareness of the qualitative. A prototype is a laboratory for exploring and refining material, tectonic and environmental qualities. Far from being merely a technical exercise about how to fasten a joint or test loading capacity, the success of a prototype is determined in part by the intensity of the qualities it exhibits.

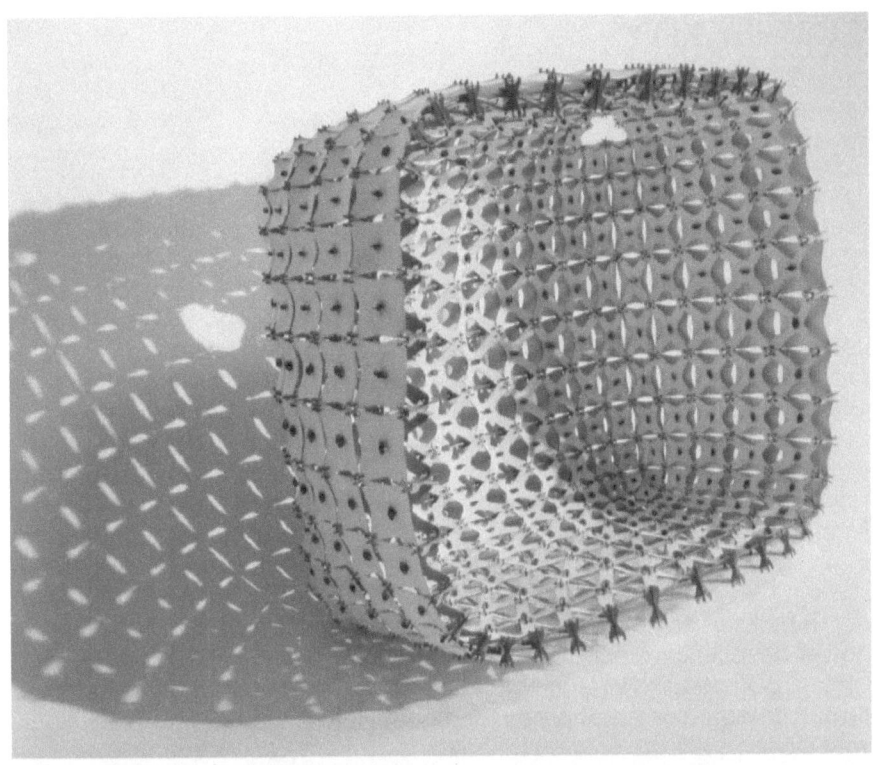

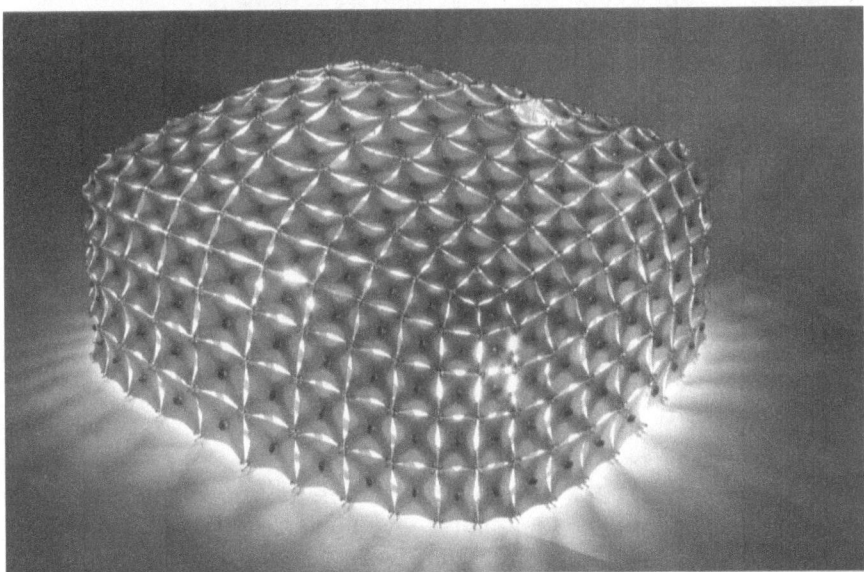

6 Structure and cladding study, paper and wood

Embracing the Qualitative

COMPLEXITY

Through a long series of experiments involving pendulums, inclined planes and free falls, Galileo discovered that the path of a projectile such as a cannonball has three component forces acting on it: a horizontal push and a vertical upward push exerted by the canon combined with a vertical downward push of gravity. Together they produce a parabolic trajectory. By measuring the component forces, Galileo predicted where the cannonball would strike, but there were actually more forces acting on the cannonball, which made the predictions only approximate. For instance, the wind exerted a fourth force, which pushed the ball away from its parabolic trajectory. The wind changes speed and direction, and Galileo had no way to measure it. In light of this situation, he did something remarkable. He ignored the wind. By measuring three of the forces involved, he explained most of the ball's behavior, and his equations achieved a useful predictive power despite their incompleteness.

This established a principle of scientific method: In order to formulate equations that predict the behavior of Nature, scientists work with closed systems of known variables. If some aspect cannot be measured, it is bracketed off, designated as a "black box", an unpredictable contributing factor, which is not accounted for in the equations. While early scientists considered these factors ripe for further study, assuming that later generations would eventually measure them, by the early 20th century many scientists assumed unmeasurability. Black box phenomena were considered chaotic, meaning that they possessed no predictable, measurable behavior. They were disregarded as inherently disorderly.

In the 1960s some scientists became dissatisfied with this view. They believed that the universe is orderly without exception, and they were not willing to ignore chaotic phenomena any longer. They saw value in discovering the underlying order of chaos. If they could do this, it would open grand new scientific territory. They could predict the weather, harness the power of static electricity, and make airplanes impervious to turbulence [2].

When they looked closely at these phenomena, they began to uncover patterns of behavior, an order. However, it was an order unlike that exhibited by a cannonball, a pendulum or the orbits of the planets. Orderly phenomena had always previously exhibited a repeating pattern. When a planet completes one revolution, it begins another in a cycle. In light of such repetition, which was prevalent especially in astronomy, scientists assumed that all order had to be in the form of repeating patterns. The central discovery of Complexity Science is that the order of the universe also includes non-repeating patterns.

A *non-repeating pattern* is one that exhibits non-random characteristics, yet never exactly loops. Your life is a non-repeating pattern. You make choices and take actions that look very different from randomness, and yet you never start over; your life is always proceeding forward into new territory. It is both orderly and (to some extent) unpredictable. The same kind of order exists in phenomena such as weather systems, animal population growth, species evolution and economies.

Complexity Science has changed the way scientists view the world, and this view is beginning to affect our culture. Designers and intellectuals in every field work to understand what it means for human life. What does it mean if order drives every aspect of the universe? What does it mean if our old conception of order is wrong? The order of the universe can no longer be convincingly embodied in the rigid and pure geometry that dominates architectural history or the monotonous repetition of orthogonal frames characteristic of the Modern era. Nor can it be convincingly characterized as arbitrary, as was popular in the decades of Post-Modernism, expressed in the juxtaposition of strange forms in the fashion of collage. Order is simultaneously more dynamic and pervasive.

The cultural shift is just beginning. Complexity has been traditionally shunned as complicated, convoluted, expensive and inefficient. In contrast, simplicity is still often assumed to be universally good, sought in everything from software interfaces to cooking recipes to lawn mowers. Simplicity is taken to be virtually synonymous with intelligibility. To make something clearly understandable, we are taught, is to make it simple. The value of simplicity is still considered by many to be beyond debate.

As the cultural shift unfolds, people are beginning to see that simplicity is not universally desirable. Simplicity in art is often boring, offering little to stimulate the mind. The assumption of simplicity in science has often led to false laws. Nature, after all, is complex. Aided by a new view of complexity, people are beginning to see a culture guilty of the error of over-simplification on a massive scale. The unmitigated pursuit of simplicity has led whole disciplines to a dead end, as in the pre-packaged food industry, the call for transparency in software interface design, and the international style in architecture. Now, introduced to an improved concept of complexity, disciplines are breaking free from the chains of minimalism.

There is nothing complicated about complexity. Once the derogatory associations fall away, it is a straightforward concept. *Complexity* is the state of being composed of many interconnected parts. While this is easy enough, two aspects of complexity require special consideration: the fact that complex things are made of *many* parts, and *interconnected* parts. By understanding the implications of these defining characteristics, designers can understand what makes complexity tick. These aspects are studied in further detail ahead.

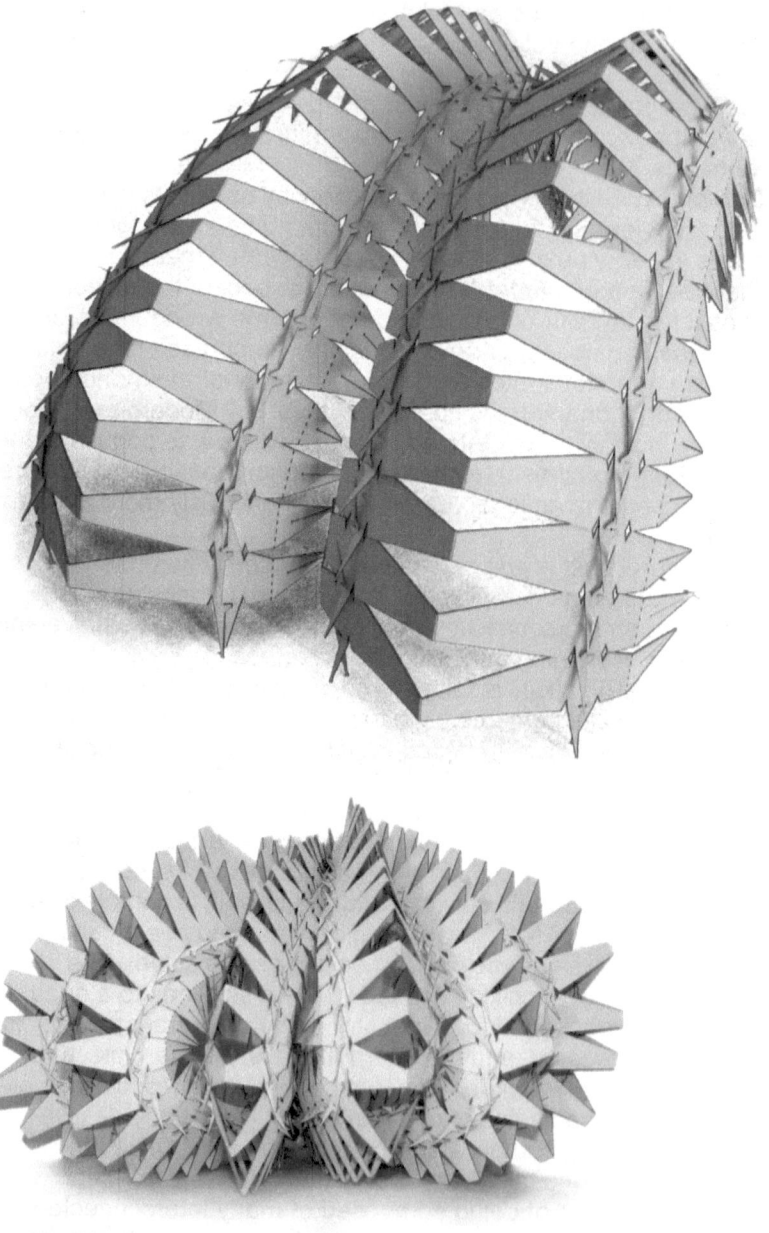

7 Structural study, museum board

Feedback Loop

PARAMETRIC MODELING

As experimental designers seek greater complexity, they need a way to manage and direct it. In the Baroque era complexity was also valued, yet designers were limited by their tools. Only a genius like Guarini or Borromini could achieve intense complexity using hand-drawn plans and sections. The computer is a crucial facilitator of complex architecture. Many get this backwards, believing instead that designers pursue complexity merely because new digital tools are capable of producing it. To the contrary, technology is a human invention subject to human motives.

The technology that facilitates complex architecture is parametric modeling. Parametric modeling generates geometry based on a system of numerical variables or *parameters,* rather than a single set of fixed points in space. Through the incremental adjustment of parameters, a digital model transforms gradually through a series of intermediate states.

Consider a parametric ellipse. An ellipse possesses a long axis and a short axis. If the long axis is controlled by a numerical variable "X", then with incremental reduction of the value of "X", the long axis is gradually shortened, causing a corresponding gradual distortion in iterations of the shape (8). Not only do parameters offer enhanced control of variation, but also of interaction. If the length of the long axis is defined as "X * A", where "A" is a percentage reduction factor, then an interactive relationship is established between the ellipses. By modifying "A", each ellipse can have a unique length, and then, by modifying "X", a proportional change can affect the ellipses globally (9).

This dual power of parametric modeling: variability and interactivity, allows geometric components to be simultaneously diverse and unified. With the help of generative scripts (see later chapters), designers can grow a complex geometric system relatively quickly and with myriad parametric controls. This stands in contrast to conventional computer modeling, which requires long hours of tedious labor to produce a similar result.

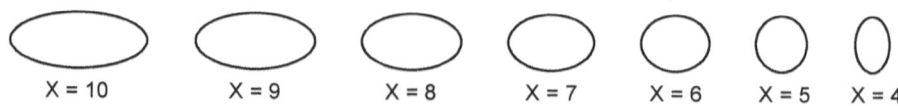

| X = 10 | X = 9 | X = 8 | X = 7 | X = 6 | X = 5 | X = 4 |

8 Iterations of an ellipse in which the length of the long axis is gradually reduced

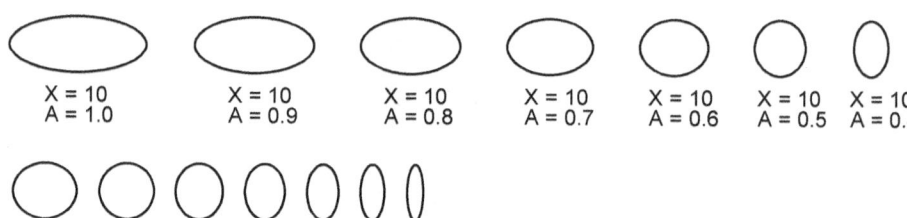

| X = 10 | X = 10 | X = 10 | X = 10 | X = 10 | X = 10 | X = 10 |
| A = 1.0 | A = 0.9 | A = 0.8 | A = 0.7 | A = 0.6 | A = 0.5 | A = 0.4 |

X = 5   X = 5   X = 5   Etc.
A = 1.0 A = 0.9 A = 0.8

9 Global adjustment of the entire system of ellipses by changing one parameter value

It is important to emphasize that parametric modeling cannot accommodate infinite variability. It incorporates variability through incrementally adjusted states of a *persistent geometric structure*. While this provides a range of possibilities and can breed high degrees of complexity, it requires the use of a class of geometry and a particular methodology. Parametric modeling methods themselves express designers' new understanding of complex Nature. Parametric modeling embodies the same kind of order and variation we see in geological systems and biological organisms. Parametric modeling requires designers to think in a way analogous to the operation of Nature, in which pattern and variation coexist.

One aesthetic implication of parametrically varied geometry is its tendency to produce non-repeating patterns and dynamic surface textures. This has become a source of inspiration for experimental designers.

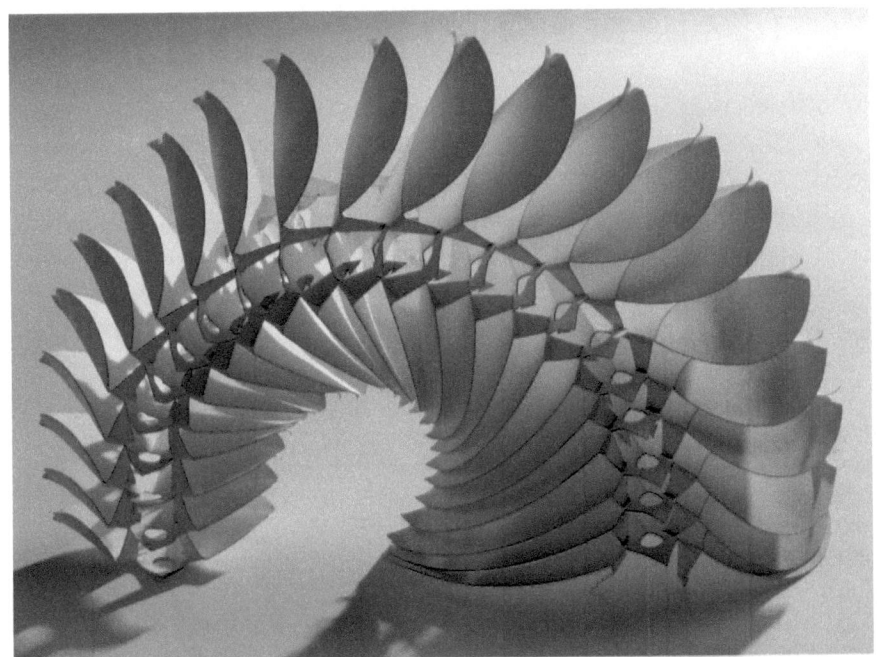

10 Structural study, cardstock paper

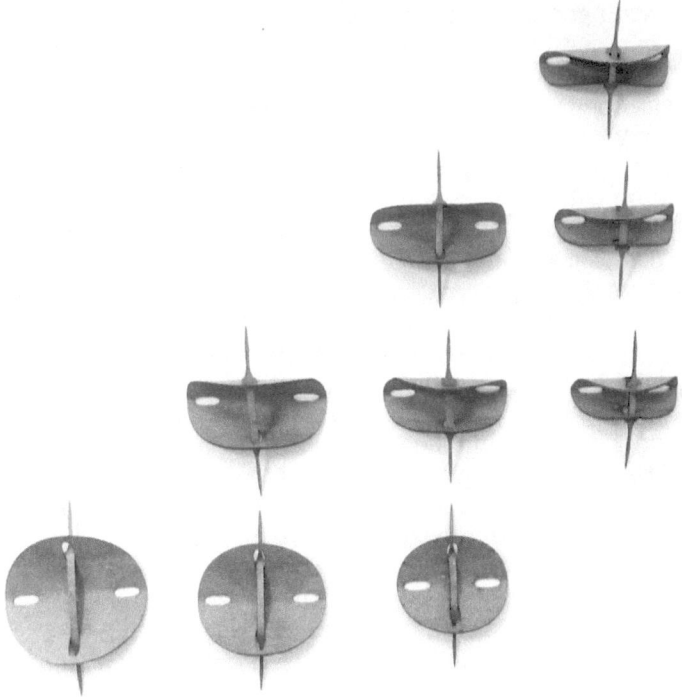

11 Tectonic study, chipboard

Parametric Modeling

BOTTOM-UP DESIGN

Designers traditionally arrive early at a desired whole, and then progressively work out the details. This is called *top-down* design. Designers define a *parti*, or select an archetype, or otherwise identify a shape for the whole, and then they work out site planning issues and programmatic massing, they develop plans and sections, they choose materials and develop wall sections, and so on down into the details. The top-down approach has advantages, but it also contains biases that experimental designers now question. Top-down assumes that geometry gets imposed on material, forcing it into a preconceived shape without concern for the identity of the parts. This is an expression of the traditional Platonic view of order in the universe, in which an unseen world of perfect geometry, of forms without content, imposes order on material things.

In light of the new view of order offered by Complexity Science, designers are changing their approach. They are rebalancing top-down with bottom-up. *Bottom-up* design starts with the details or with some simple component parts, and aggregates them together in a way that allows an orderly pattern to emerge. Instead of imposing a pre-conceived shape, a whole grows out of the parts and their interactions. Designers still control the result, but in a radically different way. If they do not like the whole that emerges, they do not change it directly. Instead, they redesign the rules or the components to operate differently, span differently, connect differently, etc. By changing the properties of the parts, they acquire new capacities, allowing them to grow into a different kind of whole.

Bottom-up thinking is influencing disciplines from architecture to genetic engineering to robotics. In the 1980s the field of robotics was throttled. Robots were still incapable of performing everyday actions such as walking or collecting objects. Inspired by discoveries made in other fields using the principles of Complexity Science, some robotics engineers began questioning the premises at the foundation of their discipline. They had assumed that the "body" of a robot had to be controlled by its "brain" (i.e., its control program), and that all behavior had to be explicitly programmed in top-down fashion. This made it difficult to perform tasks like walking, because walking is a complex behavior requiring continuous adaptation to an environment. Without the ability to pre-program all the things a robot might encounter, any new obstacle proved fatal. Some Swiss researchers took a different approach. Instead of assuming that a complex control program was needed to deal with complex environments, they used simple control programs. They let "simple-minded" robots loose in an environment to see what kind of behavior emerged. Amazingly, the robots exhibited sophisticated behaviors.

A classic example is the Swiss clustering robot [3]. The task of moving objects together into groups or "clusters" had eluded engineers. The Swiss researchers solved the problem with the following rules: 1) place two optical sensors on the front of the robot pointed outward at 45 degree angles, 2) move forward as long as nothing registers on an optical sensor, and 3) when something registers on a sensor, back up a little and then move forward again in a new direction. If a robot with only these rules/features is placed in a room of randomly distributed foam blocks, it will push them into a cluster. A complex behavior is achieved with a handful of simple rules. This principle of bottom-up design has revolutionized robotics, and it underlies sophisticated behaviors seen in contemporary robots, such as running and playing soccer.

Fueled by the principles of Complexity Science, genetic theory and atomic theory, attention is shifting away from the *whole* to the *part* as the fundamental driver of the universe. After all, the form of a sunflower is determined at the cellular level. Its form grows incrementally according to the properties of its cells (i.e., its DNA). The cells of a rabbit are different, and they grow into a different kind of whole. Bottom-up design involves the production of biomorphic patterns that possess a special combination of qualities. They are varied while possessing a sense of unity, like a sunflower or a rabbit. Bottom-up design is a technique for capturing in a man-made object the complexity exhibited by natural things.

There are two important laws of bottom-up design: 1) the Law of Simple Building Blocks, and 2) the Law of Emergence. Each applies to a wide range of natural phenomena as well as the act of design.

Law of Simple Building Blocks

The Law of Simple Building Blocks states that complexity arises naturally when simple components propagate according to simple rules. The mathematician Stephen Wolfram[4] performed experiments to demonstrate this in which he generated complex geometric patterns from a few squares in a simple initial arrangement. Complexity arises in any system where a large number of components interact, even if they interact according to simple rules.

The Law of Simple Building Blocks makes the design of complex things manageable. If complexity had to be generated directly, it would overwhelm our capacity to grasp, define and produce it. Instead, designers build up complexity out of simple units, which are controlled with simple rules of propagation and interaction. These simple building blocks provide an accessible intermediary state through which designers influence the growth and adjustment of complex systems.

Law of Emergence

According to robot scientist Josh Bongard, "...*emergence* designates behavior that has not been explicitly programmed into a system or agent" [5]. The phenomenon of emergence is inherent in creative thinking. Every insight is an emergent phenomenon, but the Law of Emergence is wider. It occurs when the result of a planned human action is not predictable or expected. Emergence is the fringe benefit of working with complex systems. It is what a complex system does in addition to what designers planned. It is windfall behavior, acquired at no extra cost and with no extra effort. It often transforms our perception and application of a system, and reveals hidden potential.

With a pure top-down approach, emergence is considered a source of error. Emergent behaviors, because they are unexpected, cause a design to deviate from designers' plans. It contaminates the purity of a parti. When designers pursue unmitigated top-down thinking, they suppress emergence to save the deductive logic of their plans.

Emergence is the generation of coherent patterns from the aggregation and interaction of simple parts. Emergence describes a property arising in a whole. It is an aspect of a whole that comes into existence without an explicit plan, but instead, through local interactions of the parts. Rules or behaviors are established for the parts, and not for the whole, and yet a coherent whole arises nonetheless. Emergence is unpredictable because it depends on a huge number of interactions, too many to track or forecast. The more interactions occur, the more pregnant a system becomes with emergent behavior.

Consider the properties of spackling compound pushed through wire mesh (12, 13, 14). What is the emergent property? Is it the plasticity or the matte finish or the viscosity of the spackling compound? These properties are well understood by materials engineers. Not only are they understood, they are deliberately accentuated to improve product performance. So again we should ask: what is the emergent property? What is really unpredicted, even by the materials engineers? It is the *visual quality* of the surface that emerges when spackling compound is pushed through mesh. It is the visual quality itself, the sum of the luminance, texture, pattern, and color that results from known and unknown material properties interacting in a complex context (e.g., network of pushing forces, geometry of mesh, and consistency of compound). The visual effect cannot be predicted by any quantitative scientific analysis.

Feedback Loop

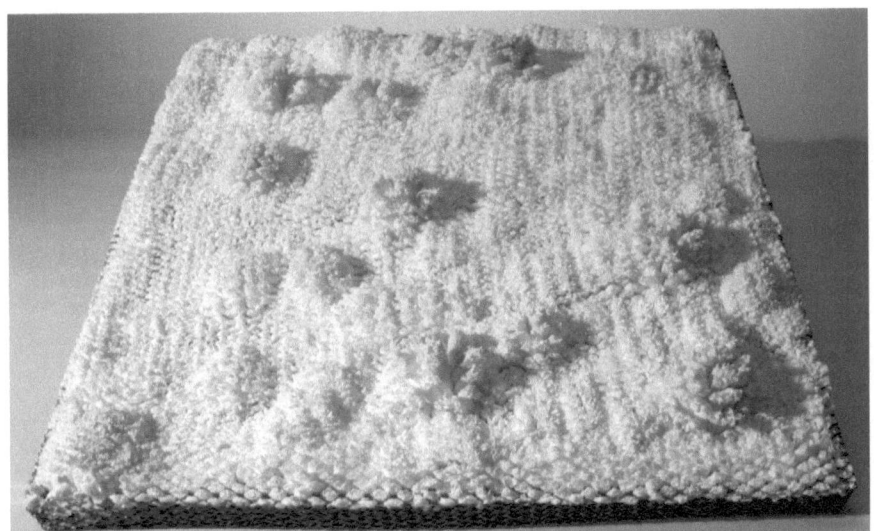

12 Cladding panel study, spackling compound, wire mesh

For designers, the search for emergence in materials is the search for emergent visual qualities that can orchestrate meaningful architectural experiences. There are quantitative aspects of spackling compound that materials engineers do not understand or have yet to even identify, but this is for them to discover. The quantitative is their realm of expertise. The designers' realm is the qualitative. When we talk about emergence, we are usually talking about emergent qualitative effects, which the methods of science and computation cannot predict.

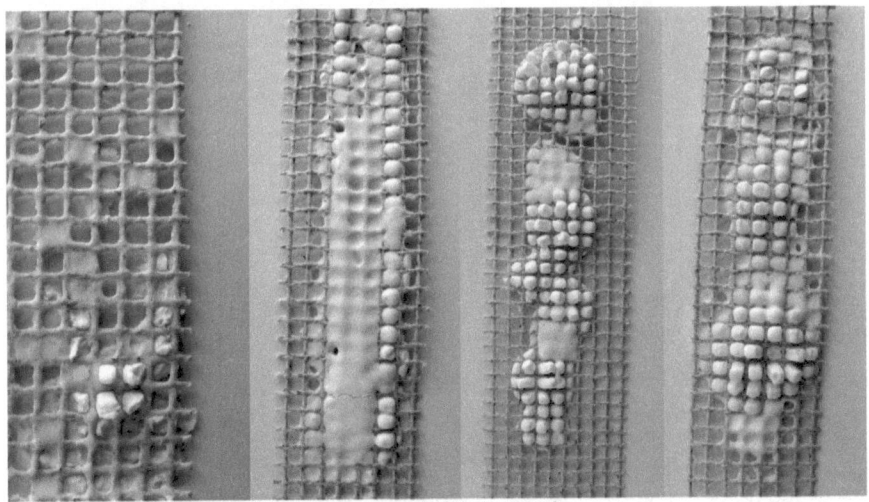

13 Material study, spackling compound, fabric mesh

Bottom-up Design

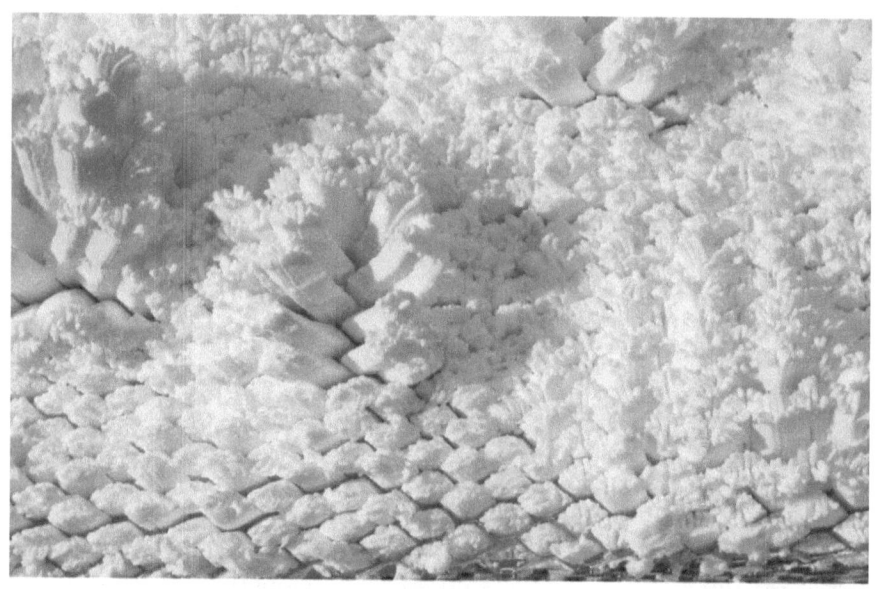

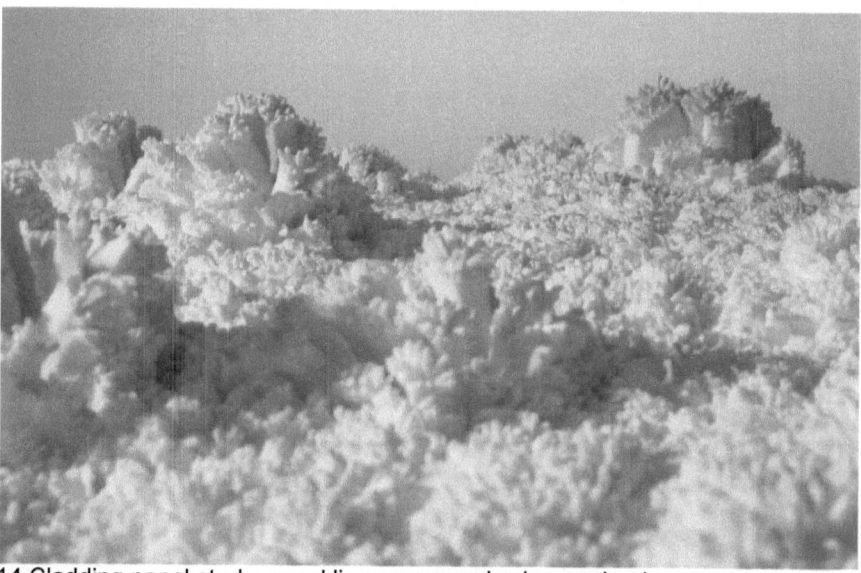

14 Cladding panel study, spackling compound, wire mesh, close up

Feedback Loop

INTEGRATION OF BOTTOM-UP AND TOP-DOWN

While it is helpful to isolate top-down thinking from bottom-up for the sake of clarification and study, it is not helpful to isolate them in design. In any healthy approach, the two work together.

After decades of formalism, which suppressed bottom-up thinking, experimental designers seek to reclaim it. Historically, bottom-up has usually been the weaker element, and so bottom-up thinking is really a new discovery. It could not be fully understood or embraced before the development of a mature concept of complexity.

The trend toward bottom-up has encountered resistance on grounds that it undermines intentionality. Bottom-up, when entirely isolated from top-down, replaces intentionality with serendipity. Pure bottom-up design is reactionary, opposed to the careful planning characteristic of top-down. In a pure top-down approach, in contrast, design becomes a matter of logical derivation, elaborating details based on a pre-established intention. Whenever top-down is pitted against bottom-up in this way, designers face a losing battle.

To reconcile them, designers negotiate with a medium rather than attempt to tame it. They coax it, herd it, nudge it in the direction they want it to go, and let it reveal unforeseen destinations that are superior to their preconceptions. This last part is especially difficult for some designers. They are receptive to the discovery of a better way to achieve their intentions, but they are not receptive to the discovery of better intentions. Allowing a material to alter one's intention seems to grant it excessive influence. In many aspects of life, people would never accept this. A driver often lets his GPS device map a route to a destination, but he would never let it select his destination. Yet in order to embrace bottom-up, designers must allow a material to reveal unanticipated destinations.

When top-down and bottom-up integrate, the steps happen roughly like this: 1) a designer develops some initial intention based on his convictions, 2) he experiments with materials to discover a latent property, 3) finding one, he evaluates it in reference to his intention, 4) if the property harms his intention, then he discards it, or, if it supports his intention, he experiments further to find ways to enhance the property, and 5) he continues this oscillation between experimentation (i.e., input from his materials) and redirection (i.e., input from his intentions), while remaining open to the possibility that his intentions themselves might need redirection as well.

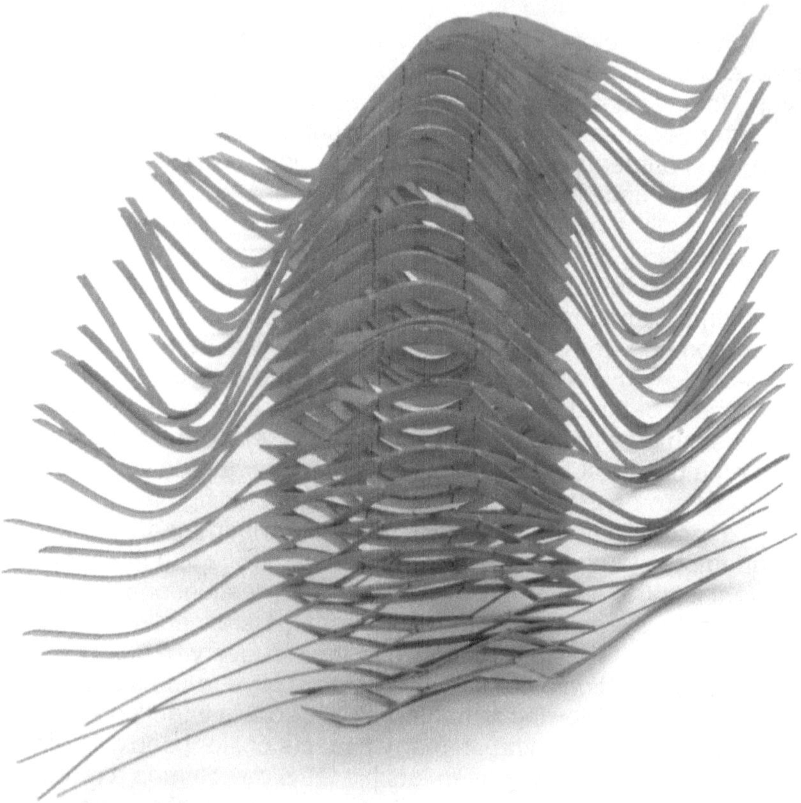

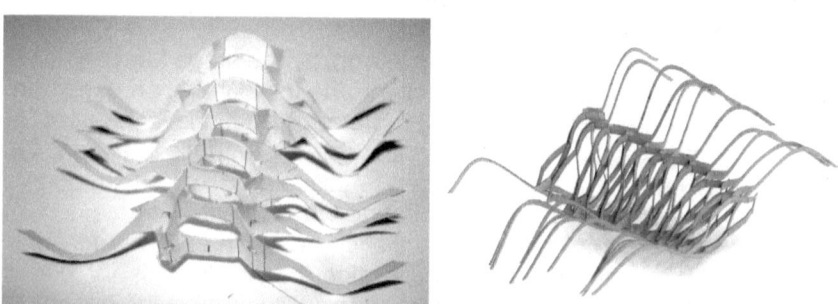

15 Structural study, cardstock paper, iterative prototypes

Feedback Loop

TAKING OWNERSHIP OF EMERGENT EFFECTS

When top-down and bottom-up integrate, designers take control of emergent effects. They do not just accept such effects in a default state, but instead, they evaluate them, and finding them desirable, they deliberately enhance them. *Emergence* is a bottom-up phenomenon, but *enhancement* is top-down. The deliberate enhancement of an emergent state is essential to an integrated process.

Enhancement involves: 1) selecting a particular aspect of an emergent state, and 2) modifying the emergent state in a way that amplifies the selected aspect. Enhancement involves the imposition of an intention onto an emergent effect through a process of selection.

Image 16 (above) shows a raw emergent effect. Batches of concrete with varied moisture and pigmentation mix to produce a "bubble" pattern, but with this effect comes undesirable side-effects. The surface is bumpy and blotchy. Image 16 (below) shows a later prototype in which the emergent effect is filtered and coaxed. The bubble pattern is accentuated while the bumpiness and blotchiness are subdued.

Materials have characteristic behaviors, but they are not purposeful. Consequently, they produce noise along with an emergent effect. Designers nurture an emergent effect by filtering the noise: quieting the effects that threaten to muddle the valued one. By adjusting a tooling process, mix ratio, heating temperature, depth of formwork, and so forth, a more deliberate version of the effect is produced.

Enhancement means to amplify, purify or intensify a raw state to achieve an intention. It involves both evaluating an emergent effect according to a purpose and intensifying the effect through deliberate modification. Designers intensify an effect by directing it toward a chosen purpose (not always forcefully or immediately, sometimes indirectly, massaging or coaxing or herding it), and by stripping out facets of its complexity through a process of subtraction or constraint.

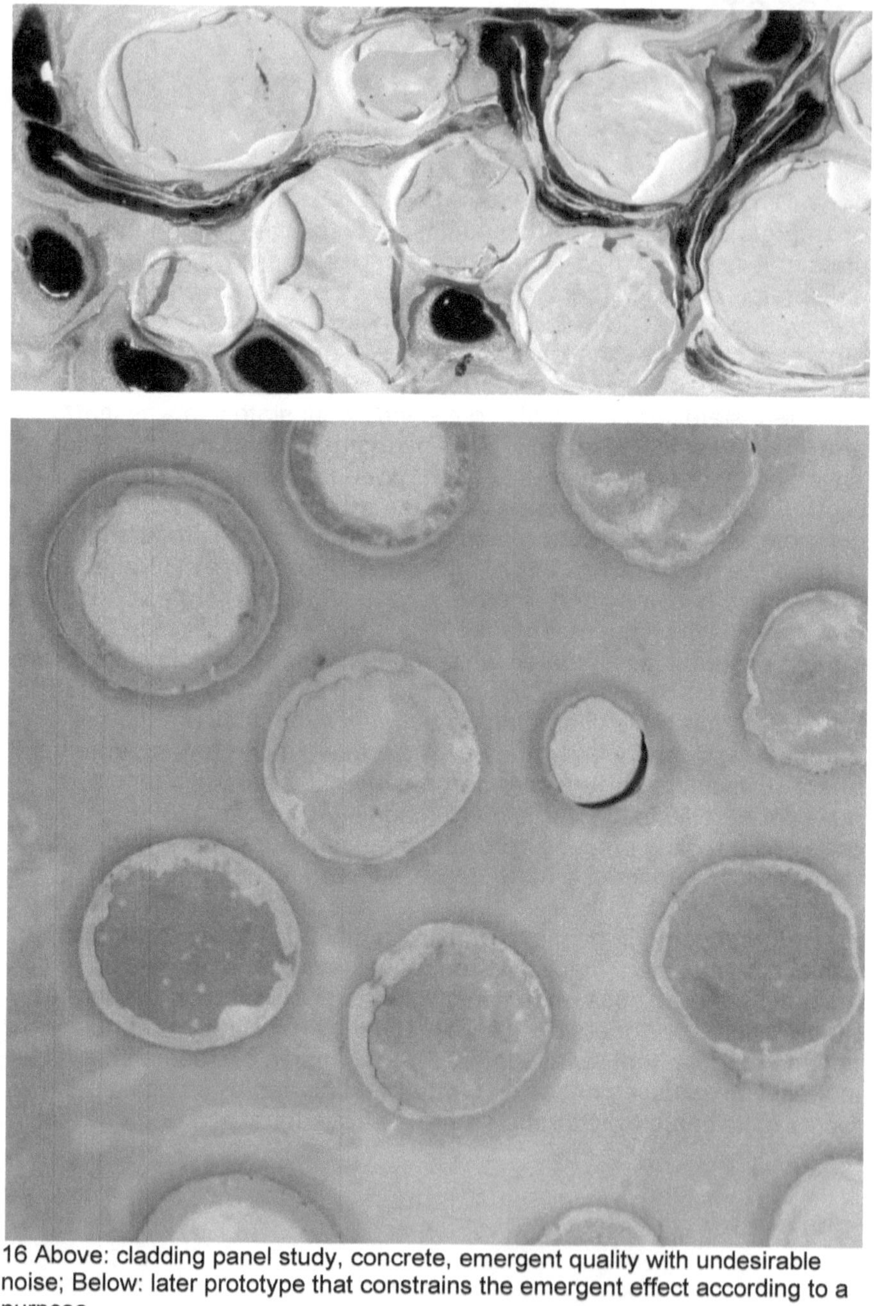

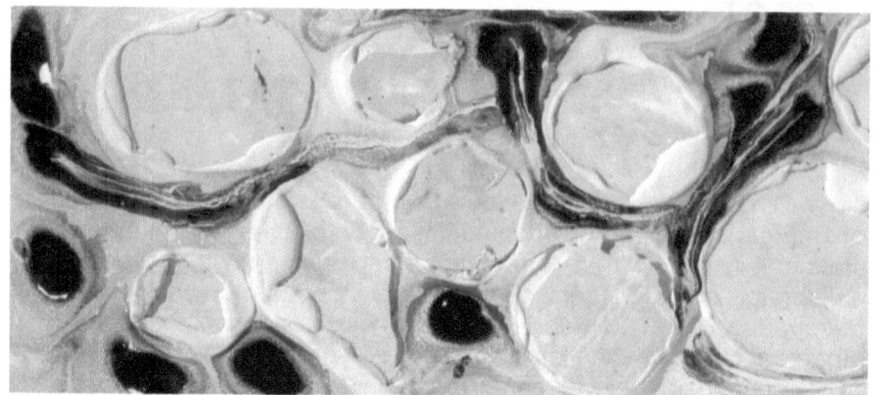

16 Above: cladding panel study, concrete, emergent quality with undesirable noise; Below: later prototype that constrains the emergent effect according to a purpose

Feedback Loop

GENERATIVE SCRIPTING

The Law of Simple Building Blocks and the Law of Emergence demonstrate that a script need not be sophisticated to produce fertile results. In fact, the most interesting scripts are often crude, yet they produce rich, diverse and unexpected results. The truth of these laws underlies the renaissance of code-writing among designers.

A *script* is a simple software program that runs inside computer-aided design (CAD) software. When a script activates, it temporarily takes control of the CAD software, creating new graphical elements or modifying existing ones according to a pre-created list of instructions. A script can generate thousands of discrete graphical elements (points, lines, surfaces, etc.) in seconds, which accelerates the construction of complex models. When a script incorporates variable parameters, its operation can be adjusted by an operator or by the script itself. This generates fields of gradually transforming elements that interact in unexpected ways.

For experimental designers, finding emergent geometric states useful in the design of complex architecture is the usual goal of scripting. This is *generative* scripting. Most generative scripts are not sophisticated enough to create a final, complete and detailed building design, and this is not their purpose. They generate provocative geometry, which can then be elaborated into a complete design by other means. Experimenting with generative scripts is the digital equivalent of experimenting with materials. By exploring a script's parameters, designers discover emergent states that act as inspiration.

Scripting is also used to facilitate such tasks as structural analysis, component fabrication and on-site construction. This is *instrumental* scripting. Rather than tap the power of scripts to breed emergent effects, instrumental scripting taps their power to organize information and automate repetitive tasks: to realize designs rather than generate them. Although both modes are creative, this book limits discussion to generative scripting. In its generative mode, scripting unleashes bottom-up thinking with unprecedented intensity.

REFUTATION OF ARGUMENTS AGAINST SCRIPTING

Scripting is the subject of much exploration, excitement and fear. While mainstream designers remain largely unaware of it, experimental designers and academics seek to understand its nature and implications. They want to understand how it supports their convictions about architecture and complexity. Given the newness of the medium, misconceptions are prevalent. Some designers ask, for instance, whether scripting is a substantial design method or a passing fad.

This chapter clarifies the nature of scripting by addressing the main points of concern voiced by skeptics. It shows the flaws of reasoning and the entrenched thinking that lie beneath their concerns. This discussion of scripting is not neutral. It provides counterarguments that seek to defeat the skeptics. It provides intellectual ammunition for designers excited about exploring this new medium. Each section addresses one of the skeptics' arguments. It presents an argument and then analyzes it.

Argument from Decorative Effects

1. Decorative effects occur on the surface of things (e.g., the floral pattern of wall paper, the fluting of a classical column, or the embroidery of a dress).
2. Decorative effects are superficial.
3. Scripting controls surface effects (two-dimensional), rather than structural, tectonic or spatial effects (three-dimensional).
4. Therefore, scripting produces superficial decorative effects of the surface.

It would be unwise to grant the validity of premise 2, which vilifies decoration, but the following analysis identifies errors regarding surface effects (premise 3), which are specific to scripting.

Error 1: Scripting Limited to Surface Effects

Some designers believe that scripting is limited to surface production, and that it biases designers against equal consideration of structure and tectonics. It is true that surface production dominated early experiments, but what designers previously chose to produce with scripts is not necessarily indicative of its full capacity. The illogic of this argument follows the form: since designers produce x with scripting, they can *only* produce x. The capacity of a technology and how its operators choose to apply the capacity are different things. Chosen applications of a technology are always a sub-set of its full capacity.

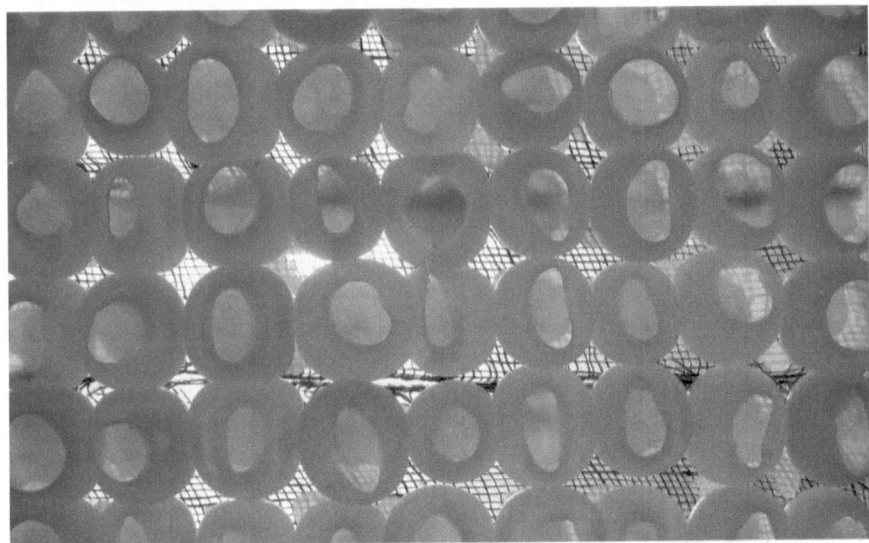

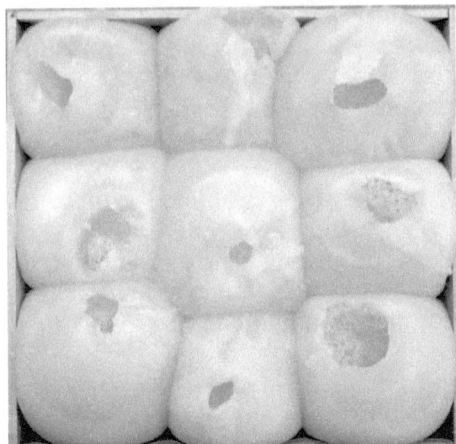

17 Above: material study, wax; Below: earlier prototype

In order to demonstrate that scripting is limited to surface effects, skeptics must show that this limitation is inherent in the nature of scripting. This cannot be demonstrated, since scripting is a generic geometry-producing capacity. It can generate geometry in a variety of user-defined ways, and it can represent any aspect of architecture including surface, structure and tectonics. As architects become more versed in scripting, the range of its applications grows beyond surface effects.

Even though scripting is not biased toward surface effects, it does have a bias, as all media do. Flat drawings were invented to represent planar, symmetrical buildings, and they continue to bias designers toward planar, symmetrical designs. Scripting facilitates the generation, depiction and manipulation of complex systems. If designers are not seeking complexity and its related features (emergence, responsiveness, diversity, etc.), then they should not write scripts. Simple, regular, repetitive things can be designed more effectively in other media.

Error 2: Scripting as Self-Referential

An implication in the argument is that a script cannot produce geometry that relates to anything outside itself. Scripting is assumed to be a formalistic game, in which the geometry is ultimately arbitrary, based on the manipulation of numbers for the sake of form-making. In this view, geometry produced by a script (or at least the distinctively scripted aspects of this geometry) have no utilitarian value. They do not relate to site or program or anything in the world, which could give them value beyond decoration.

The way a script responds to real-world factors is different from traditional media, yet skeptics assume that since it does not respond in the traditional way, it does not respond at all. Not only does scripting have the capacity to respond to external factors of site and program, it has a capacity that often out-performs traditional design methods. Scripting gains this power from its ability to construct parametric relationships.

By defining explicit parametric relationships, a script can resolve site and program relationships that would otherwise remain ill-considered. Examples include the location of a building in relation to it topography, to existing structures in a vicinity, to existing structures in a larger district, to routes of site access, to the movement of the sun, to street activity, to the turning radii of cars and trains, to views along a procession, and to the parts of a program, just to name a few. Designers using traditional methods might consider these factors too, but mostly in isolation. At best, designers might consider the interdependencies of two or three factors at a time. With scripting, on the other hand, they can examine many interdependencies simultaneously. Far from a fantasy world of form-making, scripts provide a new way to orchestrate comprehensive design, which responds to a broader spectrum of real-world concerns than would be otherwise manageable.

This aspect of scripting transforms the decorative into the performative. In performative architecture aesthetic and utilitarian aspects merge. Traditional methods often hamper this merger because they offer weak means of managing complexity. Since design involves consideration of many factors in complex relationships, designers need a way to identify and manipulate the relationships. Scripting is such a method. A network of interrelated aesthetic and utilitarian goals can be studied simultaneously and resolved together. Performative architecture is decorative and utilitarian. Every part is multi-faceted, contributing to visual and functional effects.

Argument from Professional Alienation

1. Designers specialize in creative thinking, visual thinking and qualitative thinking.
2. Computer programming is more technical than creative, more textual than visual, and more mathematical than qualitative.
3. Therefore, designers should not write computer programs, which only serve to alienate them from a design-oriented thought process.
4. Scripting is a form of computer programming.
5. Therefore, when designers need scripts, they should hire computer programmers to write them, rather than do it themselves.

Error 1: Computer Programming as Necessarily Different from Designing

A computer is a universal machine, a machine with no pre-determined purpose or method of operation. Diverse in purpose, construction and interface, it provides everything from immersive entertainment to tax preparation assistance to parametric design tools. Computation is a unique medium, vastly open-ended in contrast to traditional media. Consider the medium of drawing in contrast. Drawing is defined by *Webster's New Collegiate Dictionary* as, "the art or technique of representing an object or outlining a figure, plan, or sketch by means of lines." A singular method and singular visual product are specified in the nature of the medium.

Although computation supports a vast range of methods and products, computer programmers choose to use it in a particular way, which establishes a convention, but such conventions can be reconsidered.

The purpose of scripting, in part, is to change how we approach computation to better support the needs of designers. One of the key questions of scripting is whether it is successful in this purpose, yet the Argument from Professional Alienation asserts that there is *no possibility* of reconciliation between computation and the needs of designers. This assertion follows the false assumption that computation is a static medium with a single, persistent format, just like drawing or other traditional media.

Computation is a diverse and flexible medium. Artists, designers, scientists, and thinkers in virtually every field are only beginning to explore its potential. Scripting is an early effort.

Error 2: Only Traditional Media can Fulfill the Needs of Designers

An implication of this argument is that traditional media such as sketching, measured drawing and model-building are the only ones compatible with designing. Digital drawing and digital model-building are acceptable only because they simulate the traditional act. According to this view, computers should go no further. Scripting throws out the metaphor of hand-drawing and model-building, instead tapping the native capacities of computation, and because of this, it erodes the link between hand and eye, which is fundamental to design.

It is common for people to accept revolutionary technology only gradually, through an intermediate metaphorical stage. The medium of film was a "movie" or "moving picture". The automobile was a "horseless carriage" and then an "iron horse". Internet communication was "electronic mail" or "email". CAD software was an "electronic drawing board". Such metaphors help people transition from the familiar to the new, but to believe that a soothing transitional metaphor is the appropriate final manifestation of a technology is naive. Scripting is part of an effort to shed the shackles of metaphor and begin the real work: accessing the full power of the medium of computation in architectural design.

Error 3: The Proposed Alternative: Segregation of Designing and Computer Programming

The argument proposes an alternative approach to scripting: out-source it to professional computer programmers. This approach disregards the intimate connection that exists between designer and medium. Would it be acceptable to out-source sketching? Would sketching remain fertile if designers sent verbal descriptions to sketch artists? No. The direct, moment-to-moment interaction between a designer and a medium is crucial to the search for creative insight. Breaking the feedback loop between designer and medium leads to a top-down process: Designers come up with an idea and unilaterally convert it into a visual representation without any dialogue with the medium.

Removing scripting from the direct purview of designers reinforces the design-production split prevalent in mainstream practice. This split plagues new graduates, who often find themselves chained to production jobs in their early years. The culture of "mark-it-up and hand-it-off" should be resisted. It leads to the abuse of young professionals. If scripting becomes yet another activity segregated from designing, then it becomes another production activity, another form of technical assistance used to insulate established designers from the imperative of technology-based experimentation.

Argument from Narrow Creative Range

1. Robust design methods develop a design from concept to completion.
2. Scripting is not robust because it is only useful in the early stage of designing, to define a formal concept.
3. Therefore, at some point in a design process scripting must be discontinued so that other more robust methods can employed.
4. And therefore, the usefulness of scripting is limited.

Error 1: Scripting as Limited to Conceptual Design

The view that scripting should be limited to a particular phase of design assumes that it is limited in representational content. Consider the medium of hand drawing. Nobody would claim that drawing should be limited to a particular phase of design because drawing is a representational *method*, which does not specify what is depicted. It can represent a formal parti or a construction detail or anything else, given enough skill and time. In the same way, scripting does not specify content. Like a drawing, it can be used to represent anything, given enough skill and time.

Scripting can propagate and modify large numbers of construction components across a system. For example, designers might alter the slope of a glass roof, requiring thousands of small changes to the angles and connection fittings of mullions. Rather than endure days of manual editing of each component, a script can edit them automatically.

This power lies at the heart of instrumental scripting, which is the counterpart of generative scripting. Generative scripting happens early in a creative process, and once a design takes shape, instrumental scripting facilitates refinement, documentation, fabrication and construction. When used together, generative and instrumental scripting provide a comprehensive medium.

Taking this point even further, scripting provides a means to engage detail-level design earlier. Componentization and tectonic studies are not traditionally part of conceptual design. Detail-oriented considerations come later, after overall form, siting and program layout are decided. This devalues tectonic development by making it reactive to earlier decisions. Scripting, on the other hand, allows designers to engage details from the outset, which encourages sustained dialogue between volumetric and tectonic scales of design.

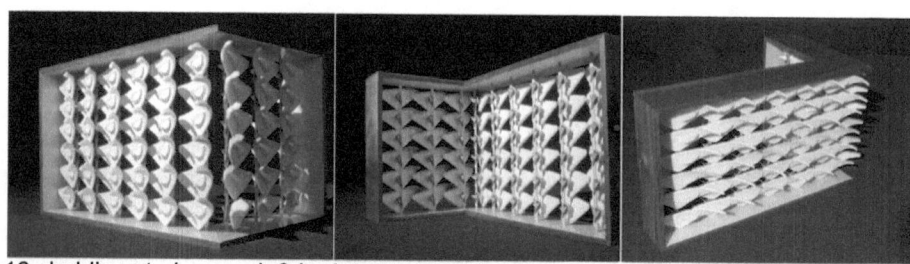

18 cladding study, wood, 3d print

Feedback Loop

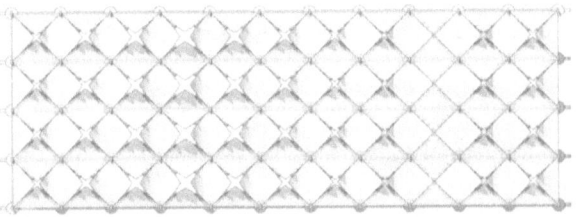

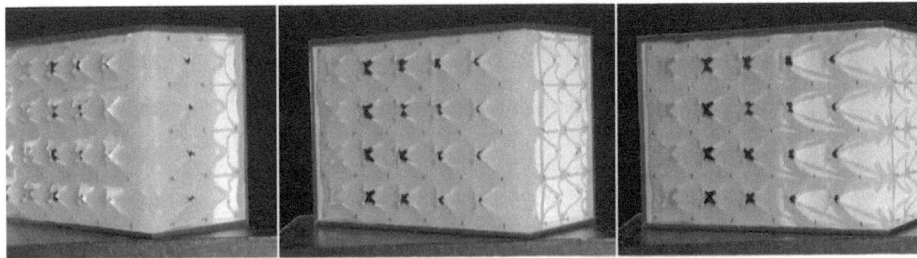

19 Cladding study, wood, 3d print and vellum

Error 2: Scripting as Incompatible with Other Design Methods

Proposing of a "cut-off point" for a medium implies that it is incompatible with other media. In this view scripting obstructs the effective use of other media such as digital drawing and model-building. To stop this from happening, scripting must be discontinued at some point in order to get out of the way. This is a false view. Scripting does not bar designers from using other media in conjunction with it.

Designers traditionally cycle iteratively through a collection of media: sketching, then drawing measured plans and sections, then sketching, then building a model, etc. Scripting is another medium in this revolving set.

When digital drawing and model-building first became available, many designers resisted. They were wary of how digital media would affect their interaction with established media. Digital media seemed so different, and these designers feared that fluid translation between old and new media would be impossible. Today, most young professionals and students find this baffling. They have no difficulty linking hand and digital media. They move fluidly between them.

Each medium has its special character, a unique set of advantages and disadvantages. Each medium opens a different window on the creative process, revealing some aspects of a design, and obscuring others. No single medium is sufficient. Only by cycling iteratively through a collection of diverse media at a quick pace can designers maintain a multi-faceted perspective. Scripting offers a new window with unique advantages and disadvantages.

Argument from Loss of Creative Control

1. Designers retain control of authorship by retaining control of design decisions.
2. Scripts automate design decisions.
3. Therefore, scripts undermine authorship.

Error 1: Automation is an All or Nothing Condition

The Modern concept of automation, based on the mass-production of standardized parts, minimizes consumers' options. Mass-production breeds large quantities of identical units. It is uniform and non-responsive. It forces one design on everyone, whether it is a coffee mug, an automobile or an apartment unit. Options only emerge in a market with multiple producers, and options are few.

Automation in script-writing does not work this way. A script is a set of responsive and interactive rules about geometry production. Scripts generate a range of results, each of which can respond to influences such as: 1) a physical context, 2) relationships between components in a building system, 3) interactions with geometric "control lines" or other control geometry supplied by a designer, and 4) numerical parameters controlling attributes such as density, thickness, smoothness, alignment, and undulation. These controls are not characteristic of Modern mass-production. Scripting uses a different kind of automation.

Automation is the self-acting or self-regulating aspect of a process. A pure automation process allows decision-making only in its start conditions. Everything else follows deterministically. Modern mass-production approaches pure automation, but script-writing is only semi-automated. Scripting combines decision-making with self-regulating behavior.

When combined with decision-making control, automation offers great value. Consider pottery. In its earliest form, pottery relied on hand-molding, but later spinning was introduced. Spinning involves shaping clay into a pot while it sits on a rapidly spinning tabletop. Pot-spinning is a semi-automated process. The pot-maker relinquishes to automation some decisions about the pot in exchange for greater control of its section curve. The section curve is controlled by pressing the clay as it spins, changing its shape. Most other aspects of the pot are automatically derived from this pressure, according to the self-regulating motion of the tabletop. If one were to suggest to a pot-maker that the spinning technique *takes away* design control, he would be baffled. In fact, pot-spinning opens new territory. The automated tabletop suppresses variables the pot-maker wants to suppress, and it simultaneously augments control of variables he wants to control. In other words, it offers a balance of automation and decision-making control consistent with his goals and interests. Scripting does the same, except that the allocation is customizable, able to be re-defined according to a designer's purpose for each script.

Error 2: Scripting is more Automated than Hand Media

Some designers believe drawing or model-building by hand is an un-automated process, which yields complete decision-making control, but this is rarely true. When designers build a study model out of cardboard, they engage in a semi-automated process. When they build a model of a wall, for instance, they retain decision-making control of its extents, but other aspects follow from an automated production process at the cardboard factory. Color, texture and planarity of the material are mass-produced. Like the pot-maker, however, most designers accept this without complaint because decisions regulated by the cardboard manufacturer are consistent with their goals and interests. On the other hand, designers making a double-curved skin might find cardboard frustrating, since the same regulated features thwart them. Measured drawing is the same. As long as designers seek architecture made of predominately straight, orthogonal edges, flat planes, and simple overall volumes, this kind of semi-automation does not hinder.

Most hand media, with their characteristic production processes, are semi-automated. The degree of automation is irrelevant. The relevant questions are: "Which features are being automated, and are they compatible with a designer's current creative goals?"

In hand media, automated features are built into the medium. Designers either accept these features or discard the medium. If planarity is not desirable, for instance, then a designer should avoid cardboard. Scripting has an advantage in this regard. In a script, designers choose what they control, what they automate, and how they do so. Scripting gives designers direct oversight of the balance of control and automation. For this reason, it could be argued that scripting offers a sort of meta-control absent from hand media.

Error 3: Scripting Limits Decision-making Control to Bottom-up

A concern raised in conjunction with this argument is that scripting supports only bottom-up thinking. The concern is usually voiced as a hypothetical design scenario. "Let's say a script generates a field of geometry, and I like most things about it, but I just want to change its overall proportions a little bit. Can I change it directly, in the model, or do I have to change the parameter values in the script and generate a completely new field of geometry?" Scripting seems to offer no way to override a pure growth process from part to whole.

The misconception that scripting is a one-directional process moving from part to whole might spring from two sources. First is a widespread interest in bottom-up thinking among experimental designers, who are often proponents of scripting. Second is strong support for bottom-up thinking in scripting. These connections between scripting and bottom-up create the appearance of a bias toward bottom-up. Additionally, the process of learning scripting often begins with bottom-up methods. Designers learn how to propagate parts according to simple rules and only later learn how to directly influence a whole. The current proliferation of work produced by beginning-level script-writers from practically every school of architecture shows a bottom-up bias for these reasons.

Despite appearances, scripting provides equal support for bottom-up and top-down. An example of a popular top-down method used in scripting is a control line. A *control line* is a line or curve that regulates the behavior of an entire system of scripted components. Designers position a control line wherever desired, and it then influences the position of components. By adjusting a control line, designers adjust the composition as a whole. In the example script shown in Image 20, designers draw a shape to designate the extents of a louver system (left). Next, they draw a line to designate where louvers have maximum openness (middle). The script then generates or modifies the louvers, calculating their degree of openness relative to the control line (right). By moving the control line thereafter, the openness of louvers adjusts globally.

Feedback Loop

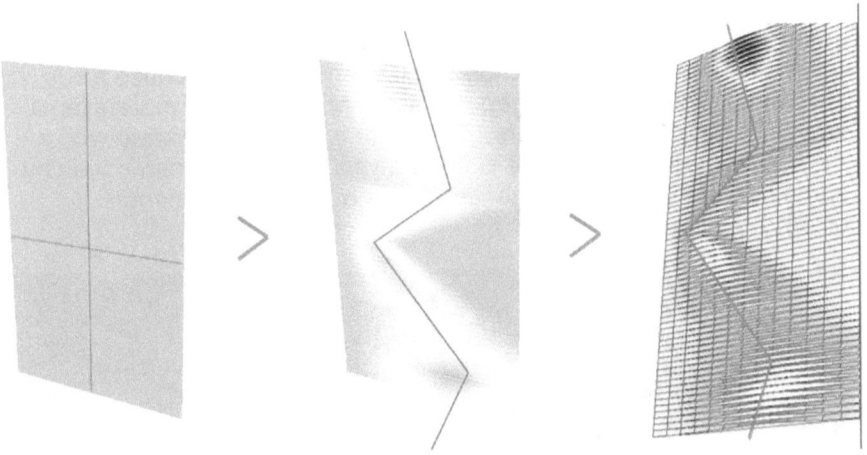

20 Process diagram of a louver-generating script

Just as scripting offers a customizable balance of automation and decision-making control, it also offers a customizable balance between bottom-up and top-down. A script can combine them, which provides bi-directional influence between parts and whole. This is another advantage of scripting over hand media. Hand media do not provide good bottom-up control. (This is one reason top-down thinking has dominated architectural history.) Scripting offers designers a balanced tool.

Error 4: Scripts Make Design Decisions on Their Own

Some skeptics remain unfamiliar with the Law of Simple Building Blocks and the Law of Emergence. When they see a script start with simple inputs and generate a complex result, they assume that the script makes intermediate decisions needed to bridge the gap. In other words, they believe that scripts operate using artificial intelligence, making decisions independently of a script-writer. While this is the most naïve misconception discussed here, it reveals a deeper source of resistance to scripting.

A script has no intelligence. It follows a list of instructions. The only difference between a script and a pencil in this regard is that a pencil cannot be pre-loaded with instructions. Instead, instructions have to be sent one at a time. A designer's hand conveys the instructions, incrementally altering direction, pressure and rotation. In contrast, a script sends a string of instructions at once. A script is no less under our control than a pencil. The power to pre-list instructions and send them at once is a useful new power, but it is not a form of intelligence.

Refutation of Arguments against Scripting

Scripts seem to have a mind of their own because they produce emergent effects, and perhaps this is what skeptics find ominously artificial. To those with a top-down bias, emergence is cause for suspicion. The more emergence a script produces, the more alien it seems to top-down designers. The more it seems to operate with a mind of its own. Emergence is not a mystical phenomenon driven by some sort of invisible intelligence. It is a natural phenomenon occurring in complex systems.

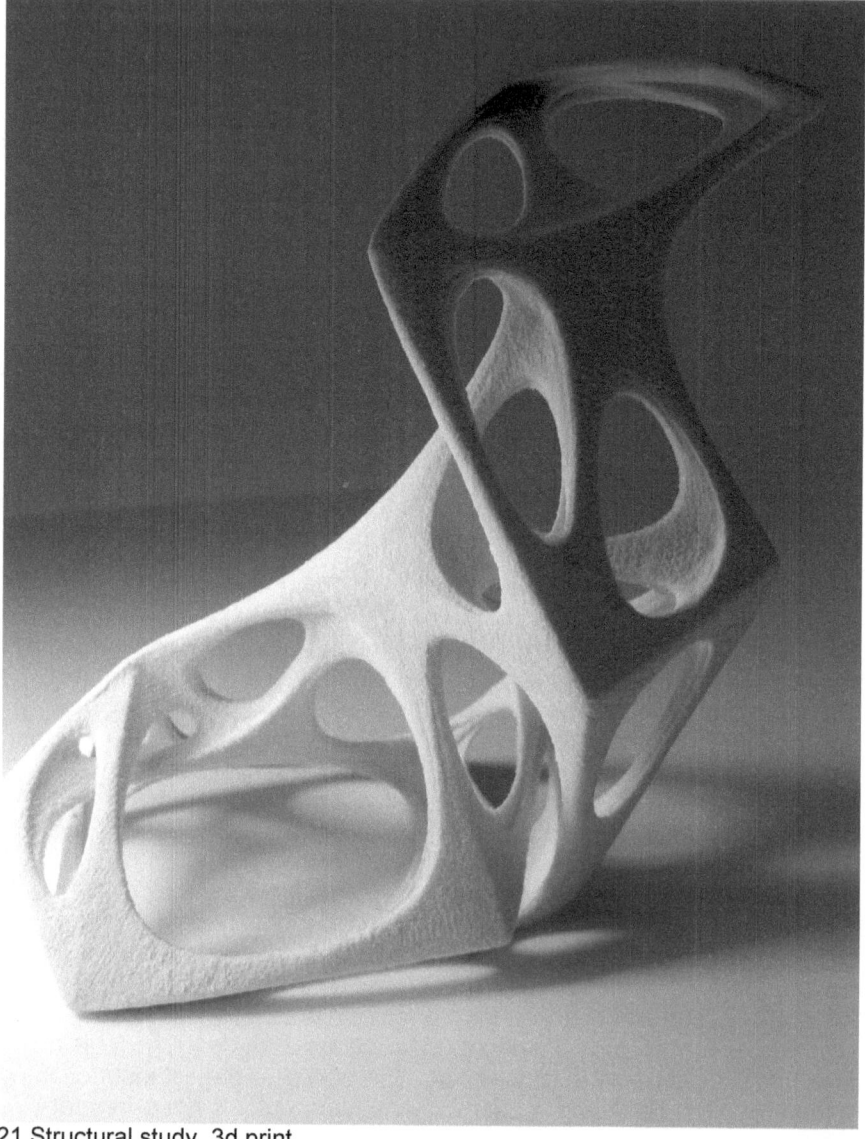

21 Structural study, 3d print

Feedback Loop

Finding Out

After Benjamin Franklin published the first theory of electricity, a skeptical news reporter asked him, "What good is electricity?" Franklin responded, "What good is a newborn baby? Wait and see." Designers should be wary of those who demand a strong demonstration of results when the experimentation has hardly begun.

Skeptics stand on the sidelines, waiting to see. From this vantage point, they lose either way. If a new idea is a flop, then they learn nothing from the experimentation. If it is a hit, then they are left behind. Rather than embrace the way of the skeptic, designers should explore. Rather than stand safely on the sidelines, they should do the testing required to reveal the consequences of new ideas. This is where we find experimental designers in their use of scripting. Those who engage scripting are excited by its possibilities, and so they explore. It is a time for innovators, not skeptics. It is a time for those who are discontent with a centuries-old design process. It is a time for those who believe they can find a better way. Is scripting part of this better way? Some will wait and see. Others will find out.

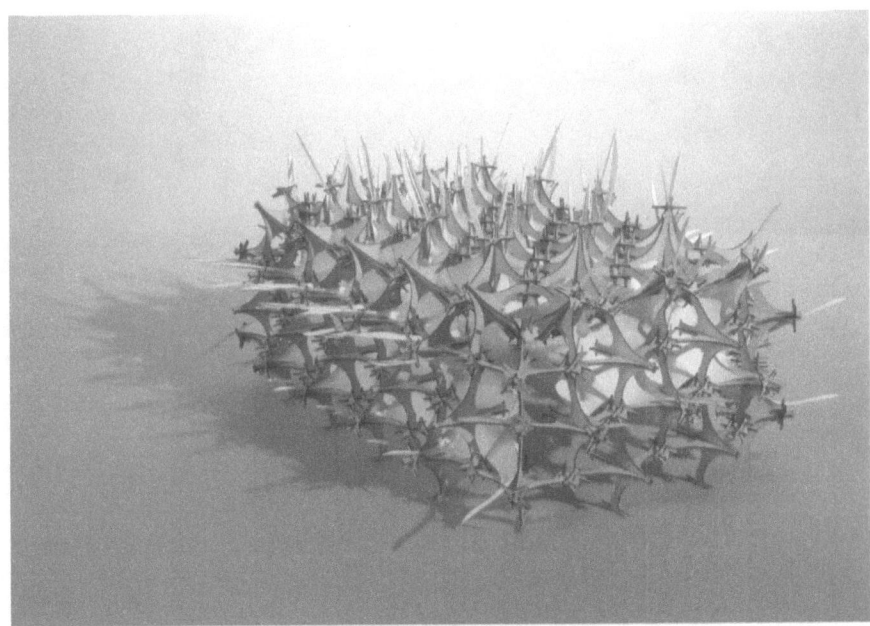

22 Structure and cladding study, chipboard and paper

SCRIPTING AND PARAMETRIC THINKING

Parametric thinking is broader than scripting. Scripting is one tool used to facilitate parametric thinking. It allows parametric thinking to thrive, and it reveals the implications of parametrically-conceived designs more quickly and completely than traditional media.

This point can be stated more forcefully. It is not scripting that is revolutionizing design; it is parametric thinking. Parametric thinking provides a new perspective on design, especially with regard to the relationship between parts and whole. It enables an integrated perspective on part-whole that has never fully existed in the history of architecture. Some designers in past ages got close, Borromini for instance, but even he was working from intuition, with no theory of complexity and emergence to guide him. We live at the cusp of an age in which the intuitions of some past geniuses are being worked out and made available to all designers as explicit and potent guiding principles.

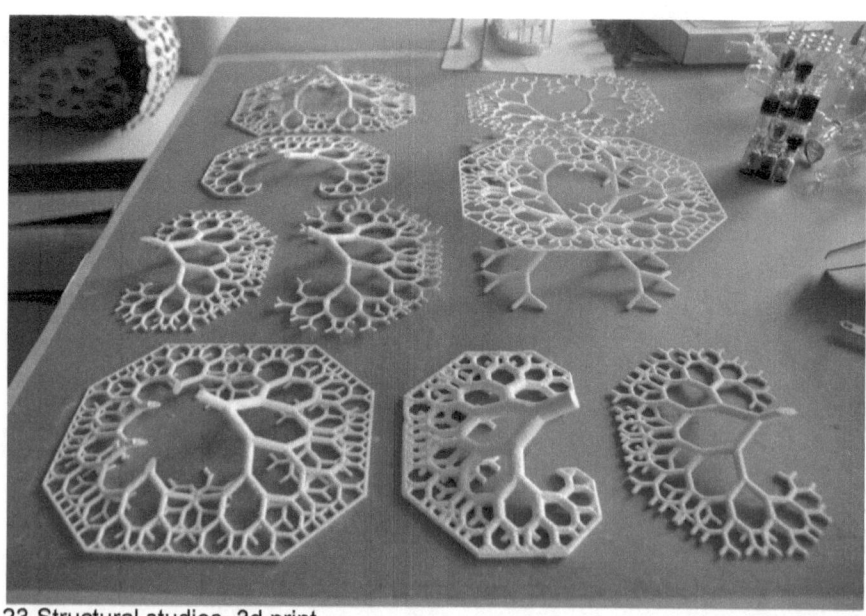

23 Structural studies, 3d print

Feedback Loop

SCRIPTING AND EMERGENCE

The Law of Unintended Consequences applies to scripting. The law states that whenever we choose a course of action in a complex context, the action produces some unintended consequences because it is difficult to forecast every chain of cause and effect emanating from the action. A classic example is the highway bypass. It is constructed to relieve traffic congestion, but it also attracts new development and with it more cars, resulting ultimately in more traffic rather than less.

Each of our actions knits into a complex world replete with interactions. Such dense networks of interacting things exist in the atomic structures of materials and the parametric structures of scripts (24). This gives scripts a similar unpredictability.

An example of an unintended consequence is seen in Image 26, where under some circumstances a branching script creates wreath-like structures instead of the intended tree structures. The script produces trees as intended, but the wreath-building behavior happens additionally, as unintended windfall behavior.

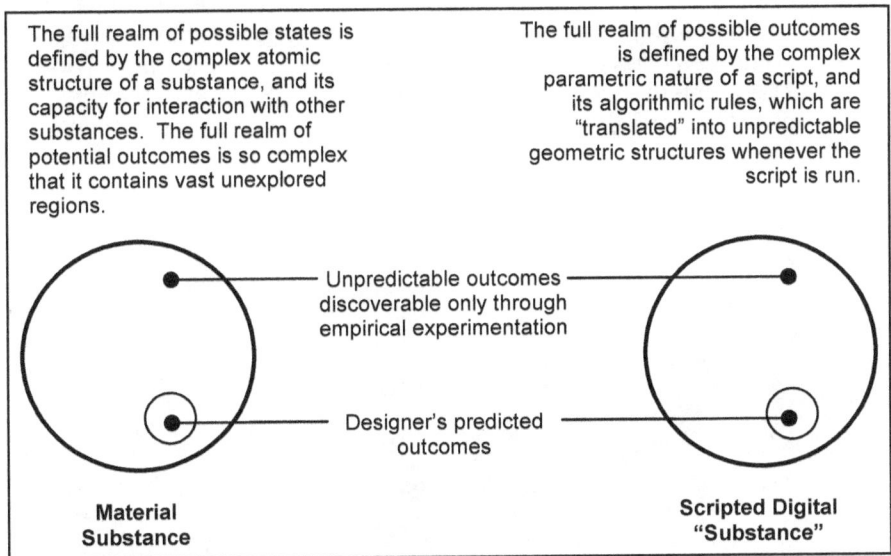

The full realm of possible states is defined by the complex atomic structure of a substance, and its capacity for interaction with other substances. The full realm of potential outcomes is so complex that it contains vast unexplored regions.

The full realm of possible outcomes is defined by the complex parametric nature of a script, and its algorithmic rules, which are "translated" into unpredictable geometric structures whenever the script is run.

Unpredictable outcomes discoverable only through empirical experimentation

Designer's predicted outcomes

Material Substance

Scripted Digital "Substance"

24 Emergence in materials and in scripts

Although emergence exists in materials and scripts, it happens differently. Emergence in natural systems such as materials, weather fronts, ant colonies, turbulent water, and flocks of birds is inherent in the medium and discovered by designers. Emergence in man-made systems such as market economies, cities, and scripts is first unknowingly created by designers and then subsequently discovered.

When a designer writes a script, he creates every aspect of it, including any emergent behavior. The potential is there when he writes it, but it is latent, just as many properties of a material remain latent in the course of its normal applications. Even though the designer put the latent potential into the script, he must discover it just as he does in a material, through a process of testing and observation. It is only when the latency emerges that he sees the unintended consequences of his script writing.

In a script with a few simple rules, the resulting emergent behavior is greater than the sum of the rules. The behavior is not arbitrary; it is entirely caused by the rules, but it is nonetheless unpredictable. Emergence is not an exception to the Law of Cause and Effect, it is a form of cause and effect, a form characteristic of complex systems.

For some well-studied natural systems like the weather, scientists might eventually discover underlying causal interactions, entirely unknown today, which allow them to predict its behavior (given adequate computational power). In the case of weather, this would mean the ability to predict the precise time and location of a rain cloud. This is not likely to happen with the complex systems designers create. Just like the weather, such systems can theoretically be understood fully, but no matter how advanced science becomes in this analysis, it is not a process designers would care to apply to their scripts. The benefits of emergence do not require designers to understand the causal interactions they script, only to uncover and tap the results once they are scripted.

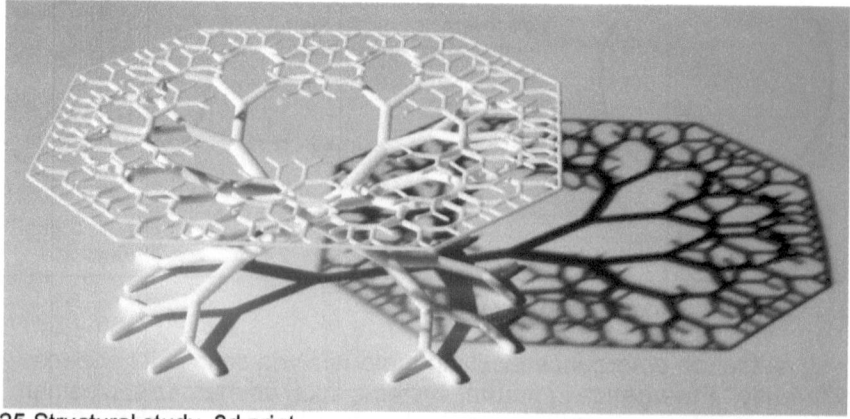

25 Structural study, 3d print

Feedback Loop

EVALUATING THE SUCCESS OF A SCRIPT

The success of a script is properly measured in relationship to the goal designers establish for writing it, yet given the nature of experimental design, this leaves them in a conundrum. As we have seen, generative scripts produce unpredictable outcomes, and experimental designers revise their goals in response. If designers do not want the output of a script to correspond to their current goal, and instead they want it to reveal something new, and if the goal will change in response, then how can they ever use the current goal as a standard of judgment to evaluate the product of a script? They seem to be going in circles.

Professionals in other fields rarely face this conundrum. When professional software programmers establish a goal for a particular module of code, they usually evaluate its performance in reference to the goal. Once established, the goal is fixed or *closed*. Using such a goal, they see unanticipated behavior produced by their code as a flaw. An example is the Surface by Section tool in a popular mainstream modeling software. In a recent version of the software this tool allowed designers to pre-select a collection of section curves by opening a selection box around them. Then the tool would loft a surface over the curves. When designers have a lot of curves, this speeds the process. Then in the next version this behavior was gone. I inquired about it with the software development company, and they said that this behavior was considered a bug, since it was not consistent with the performance specification. In other words, because this pre-selection behavior had not been intended, it was deemed a flaw. It was systematically removed from the tool, and now designers have to go through the tedium of selecting each curve individually. This kind of short-sightedness often results from closed goals. Experimental designers, in contrast, characteristically embrace the unanticipated and respond to it with enthusiasm and determination to leverage the discovery by revising their goal. This approach is characteristic of *open* goals.

Having an open goal is different from having no goal at all. When designers have an open goal, they pursue it with focus and diligence. However, they also revise it as new information and unanticipated opportunities appear. Even though it might be often revised, designers nonetheless have a clear goal at each step.

Those who think in the closed manner tend to find the open manner baffling. To them it seems like a contradiction: if you keep revising your goal, then it is not really a goal. Closed thinkers often accuse open thinkers of being uncommitted, willing to throw out a goal at the first sign of trouble. They accuse open thinkers of being impulsive or opportunistic. While some open thinkers are probably guilty of these crimes, there is nothing inherent in open thinking that requires them.

Open thinkers can also be principled thinkers who pursue convictions. Open thinkers understand the power of combining persistent long-term goals (i.e., convictions) with fluid and adaptable short-term goals, and they believe that the best way to achieve their convictions in the long-run is to responsively negotiate with the current situation.

Closed thinkers often fail to do this. The programmers who "fixed" the "bug" in the Surface by Section tool conformed to the short-term goal of making the tool perform as specified, but in doing so they deviated from the larger goal of the company to make the best tool for their customers. Fixation on static short-term goals often distracts us from larger convictions that guide and justify the selection of short-term goals.

The seeming paradox of goal-setting and goal-adapting comes from equivocation regarding two scales of goal-setting: short-range and long-range. Designers need short-range, project specific goals, which respond to a project situation. Precisely because these goals are variable and responsive, however, designers then need a second kind of goal, which transcends any specific project, and that acts as a persistent standard by which to evaluate short-range, project-specific goals. When designers adjust short-range goals, it is not a breach of their integrity. To the contrary, it is a necessary expression of integrity, since they must adjust them in order to maximize achievement of persistent long-range convictions.

Now back to the conundrum of measuring the success of a script. If a designer's long-range goal in script-writing is fresh ideas about architectural structure, surface, pattern or tectonics, then the standard by which he judges success is the degree to which fresh ideas arise. Some designers want to discover new potential in the performance of skins. Others want to find new visual qualities. Others pursue complexity or dynamism. The judgment of success is made in reference to this kind a long-term, over-arching and persistent goal, which acts as a stable compass regardless of insights gained and adaptation made in response to a particular run of a particular script for a particular project. Is there any kind of insight to be gained from a script that would lead its writer to conclude that complexity is not desirable? Or that architecture should not be performative? Or that rich human experiences are suddenly undesirable? A script, like all else, is a means to realize long-term convictions, which transcend the experiment at hand despite aggressive exploration and adaptation.

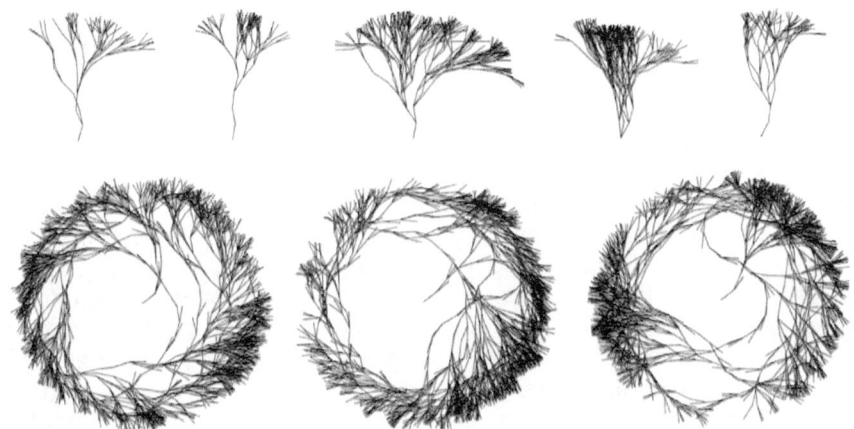

26 Scripted study, branching behavior (above) and wreathing behavior (below)

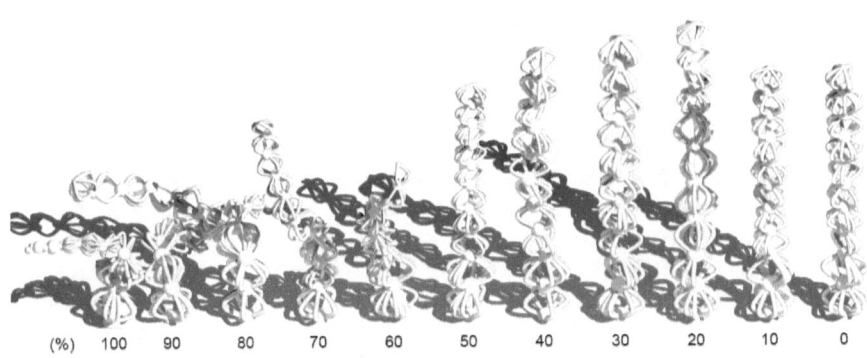

(%) 100 90 80 70 60 50 40 30 20 10 0

27 Scripted study, kelp behavior, showing degrees of suppleness

Evaluating the Success of a Script

PART AND WHOLE

Bottom-up versus top-down is closely connected to the question of part versus whole. Should designers create parts and see what kind of whole grows when those parts are propagated? Or should designers focus on creating a whole, and then fit into it whatever parts will hold it up? As we have seen, doing either makes trouble. Part and whole are integral; each should be designed with influence from the other.

Just as complex architecture involves an integration of bottom-up and top-down, it involves an integration of part and whole. In a complex system, part and whole mutually influence each other. Individual parts aggregate into a whole, but once a whole takes shape, it has an identity of its own, which can "push back" on the parts, affecting their behavior. This happens in the human body. Left alone, muscle cells grow in a certain way, based on behavior encoded in the cells. However, by challenging the body with rigorous activity such as weight-lifting, we create a feedback loop to the cells, causing them to adapt their pattern of development. A complex system develops not only as a result of an interaction among the parts at the micro scale, but through interaction of the micro and the macro. When applied to architecture, this feedback loop produces wholeness (a sense of being one orderly thing), and simultaneously it produces ubiquitous difference: variety spread throughout all the parts composing the whole. This variety maintains the identity of the parts, producing what we might call "partness".

Designers have a concept of wholeness passed down through history, but they have virtually no concept of partness. Since part-whole integration requires both a sense of wholeness and partness, the new movement often explores partness, seeking to master this less understood element.

The alternative to part-whole integration, which has dominated architectural history, is pure wholeness. In its pursuit, designers attempt to maintain the perfection of one all-encompassing idea or form. A sphere is geometric perfection because it possesses one surface. Air is perhaps the closest thing to material perfection, since it appears as a seamless continuity. In architecture pure wholeness is unattainable since construction requires the subdivision of a whole into parts to facilitate fabrication. The parts are then aggregated back together on site to make a whole, but it never again attains perfect singularity. Each part remains a discernable fragment of the whole, like the shards held together after shattering a pane of laminated glass.

The shards serve only to degrade the perfection of the pane, which would have been pristinely singular without them. Likewise, the bricks in a wall, with their grouted joints and color variation, disrupt the perfection of the wall as a whole with the distraction of visible distinctions among parts. In this view, the particularizing of a thing is a form of corruption.

When parts and whole integrate, on the other hand, it expresses a world driven by cause and effect rather than singularity. It acknowledges that the world is a complex network of particles and entities in which wholes arise as a by-product of part-to-part and part-to-whole interactions. These contrasting treatments of the part-whole relationship embody contrasting views of how the constituents of the world operate: the part as life-force and generator versus the part as corruption – the part as source of order and dynamism versus the part as source of disruption of a static perfection.

The integration of top-down and bottom-up might seem at first glance like a question of design process, which offers new avenues of creative exploration, but in fact, it embodies a view of the world. The purpose of integrating top-down and bottom-up is not merely to enhance creativity, but to enhance the creation of orderly, complex and dynamic buildings driven by the interaction of part and whole. The process and the world view underlying complex architecture cannot be separated.

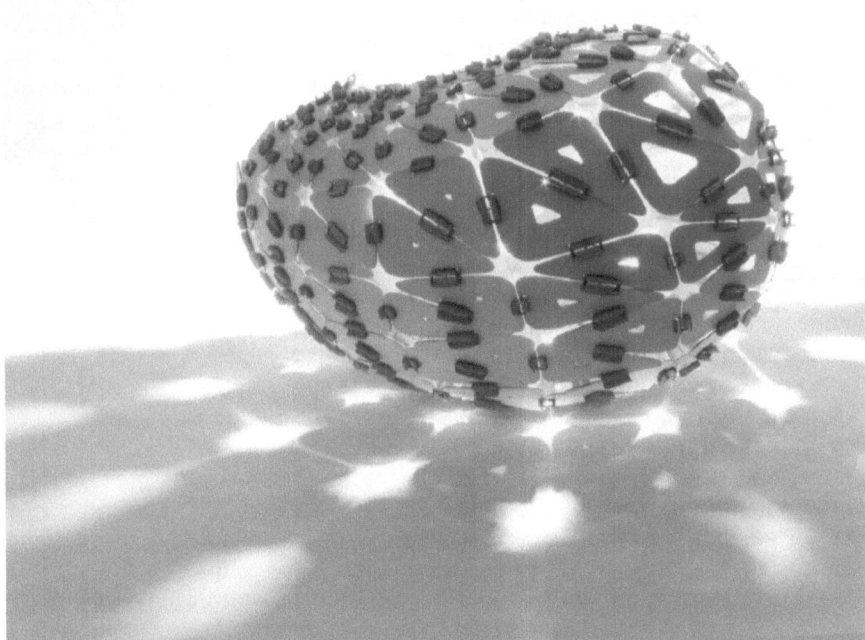

28 Structure and cladding study, museum board, rubber bands

FEEDBACK LOOP

When top-down and bottom-up integrate, they complete a circuit of creative thinking. They establish a feedback loop between emergence and intention, between part and whole. Embracing the feedback loop is the means by which experimental designers embrace complexity. The only way to interact successfully with complex architecture is through the feedback loop. Since designers cannot predict the behavior of a complex thing, they must respond to its behavior as it unfolds. They push on it, see what happens, adapt and push again.

The trouble with the concept of a feedback loop is that it suggests an oscillation between, for instance, thinking about the parts and then thinking about the whole. While oscillation is an aspect of the feedback loop, it involves more. When in the loop, designers constantly formulate a vision of the whole (i.e., they constantly think top-down). Likewise, they constantly respond to feedback from their medium, and eagerly adapt their vision to leverage new discoveries (i.e., they constantly think bottom-up).

In the feedback loop, top-down and bottom-up do not activate and deactivate at some threshold state of design development, for example, working in top-down mode until the end of Conceptual Design, then switching to bottom-up thereafter. For that matter, the feedback loop is not properly depicted as an oscillation moving however rapidly between top-down and bottom-up. Instead, the perspectives *interact*, affecting each other at every step. Interaction requires simultaneity.

Oscillation between top-down and bottom-up erodes the polarity between them, but it does not eliminate it. When designers seek the feedback loop, achieving a frequent oscillation is an admirable first step. The point here is that it is only a first step. To fully achieve the feedback loop, designers must identify a shared element, a common denominator existing in both thought processes. This shared element allows designers to see top-down and bottom-up not as opposites, but as aspects of one thought process.

To see the shared element, we need to reexamine the definitions of top-down and bottom-up. Top-down thinking brings about a desired whole, or more precisely, it realizes an intention for a whole. Bottom-up thinking, on the other hand, responses to feedback from a design context, which is used to adjust a whole, or an intention for a whole. Restated more compactly: top-down thinking involves the *pursuit* of an intention, and bottom-up thinking involves the *adaptation* of an intention. Neither process can occur without an intention.

In the traditional view, top-down holds a monopoly on intentionality, but bottom-up thinking is not random or in any way anti-intentional. Bottom-up thinking is an *aspect* of intentional thinking. It is the process of observation and adaptation that allows an intention to grow, mature and actually be realized. The key to resolving the polarity is to grasp that intentionality is impossible without both top-down and bottom-up thinking.

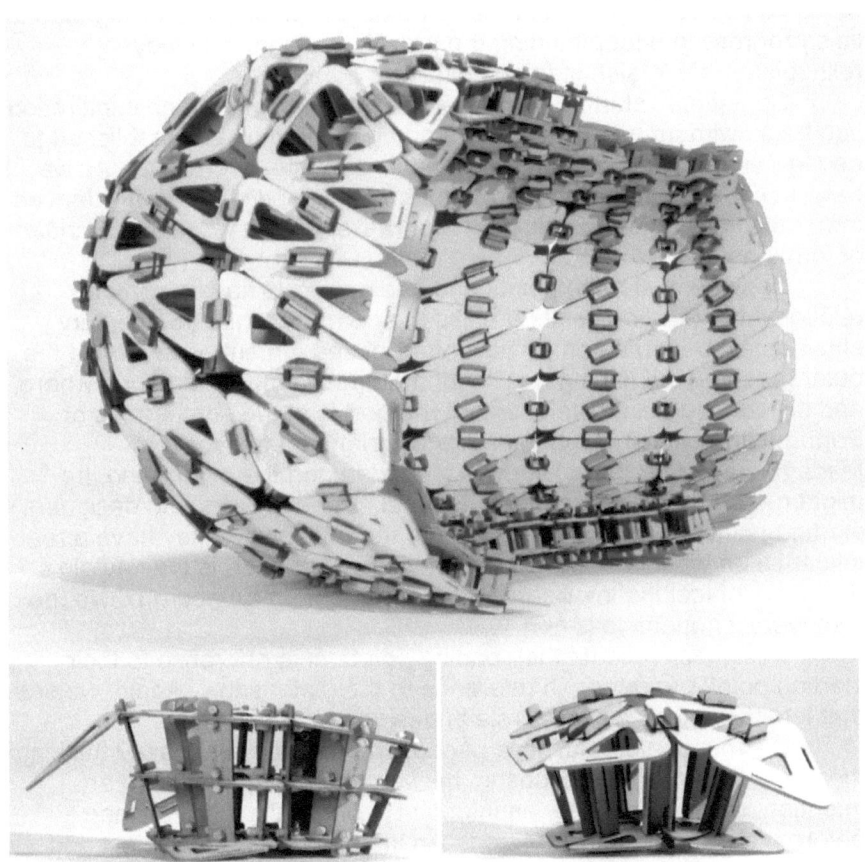

29 Structure and cladding study, museum board, rubber bands

Feedback Loop

STARTING POINTS

Early scientists believed that the material needed for plant growth came from soil and water. Since plants are made out of solids and fluids, they must have soil and water as nutrients to grow bigger. In the 18th century plant physiologist Stephen Hales discovered otherwise. He carefully weighed potted plants as they grew, and he also weighed the soil lost from the pots, and also the amount of water provided to keep the plants alive (carefully accounting for evaporation). The soil and water accounted for only about half the weight of the plant! Where did the rest of the plant come from? As it turns out, plants convert gaseous elements collected from air into material needed to build new cells. About half of plant material is made out of air. Scientists made little progress in understanding the growth of plants until they relinquished their false starting point.

Sometimes starting points can be our undoing, but no exploration can begin without a beginning. A starting point must be established to engage any process of thought, whether scientific or creative. As we have seen, creative insights are unpredictable and not logically derived from designers' starting points. If they were, design would be a matter of formulae.

Designers' starting points and ending points have a complex relationship. Starting points are like the home port of a 15th century ship captain departing on an adventure at sea. Intent on exploring the outer reaches and finding new land, the captain must start somewhere, and his starting point is relevant. If the port is at the southern tip of Portugal, the captain might discover an island off the coast of Madagascar. If he departs from Amsterdam, on the other hand, he might more likely hit the coast of Iceland. For explorers and designers, starting points provide a trajectory into the unknown. They have a real influence on what is discovered and when. However, is the captain's discovery of Iceland invalidated if he departs from Edinburgh? No, he discovers it nonetheless [6].

Designers validate their ending point *not* in reference to their starting point, but rather, in reference to their intentions. Again, we see that intentions play a central role in design.

We must be careful here. According to top-down-biased thinking, there is a one-to-one relationship between a starting point and an intention, since in this view an intention is only valid if pre-defined, before a starting point is selected. An intention is used to select and validate a starting point, and then further design decisions are logically derived from the starting point. In this way of thinking, the starting point

Feedback Loop

gives validity to all further decisions until an ending point is reached; it is the logical foundation on which the validity of the ending point rests. To change one's starting point mid-stream is to undo the logic of a design. Thus, for the top-down designer, the selection of a starting point is the most important decision; it is the lynchpin of a design. This is part of the reason careful attention is given to selection of a parti or archetype.

When the feedback loop is fully engaged, however, intentions evolve as designing unfolds. This means that a starting point necessarily happens *before* intentions gel into a final form. Thus, designers' starting points and their intentions are *necessarily different*. As with the captain, the starting point is relevant, but it is no longer properly considered the lynchpin.

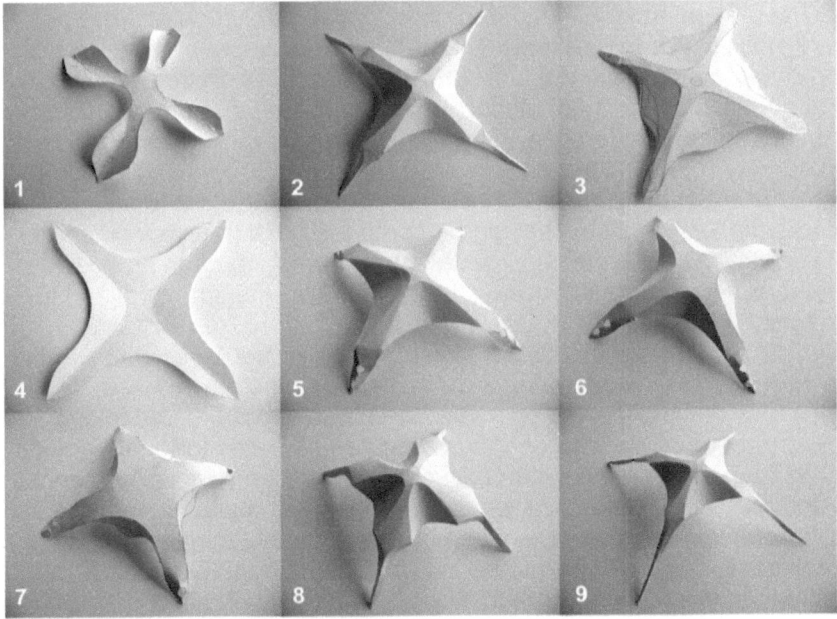

30 Iterative studies of a component, paper

BIOLOGICAL AND MAN-MADE SYSTEMS

A *system* is a coordinated assemblage of parts forming a unified whole. The concept of system is closely related to the concept of complexity. Notice the shared elements. Each involves parts assembled together, parts coordinated by means of rules or interactions, and a whole. While the concept of complexity emphasizes the underlying conditions that give rise to this kind of whole, the concept of system emphasizes the product itself. A system is the product of complexity. It is the special kind of whole that results when a large number of interactive parts congeal into a unity.

Systems have often been important in architectural thinking, but their conception and purpose has changed through the ages. The Modern conception of system involves spatial uniformity and egalitarianism (i.e., homogenization of human experience). It is implemented through serial repetition and standardization. Modern systematization was pursued in part as an expression of classical scientific method, with its impetus to analyze and classify natural phenomena and optimize man-made structures for machine-like efficiency. Post-Modern designers rejected this conception, which they accused of being sterile and dogmatic. Regrettably, the alternative they offered was the *arbitrary*, the outright rejection of systems. The new movement, in contrast, asserts a new conception of system, one that avoids the sterility of Modernism by replacing uniform sameness with incremental difference. Singularity is replaced with integrated multiplicity.

The first principle of the new conception of system is *differentiation*. Systems should be composed of a heterogeneous set of interactive sub-systems. These sub-systems are often nested together across different scales: the volumetric, the structural and the tectonic.

A second principle is *consistency*. Unlike the Modern use of the term where it is synonymous with "sameness", the new movement describes consistency as an interrelatedness or pattern underlying many incrementally different parts or states. Whereas Modern design tends to treat the relationship between parts with numerical sameness (each part is the same size, the spacing between parts is the same distance), the new movement establishes only a relational sameness. Consider a cake mix. Its molecules are bound together with a certain cohesion, which is the same throughout the mix, but this degree of cohesion nonetheless allows each particle in the mix to change its position relative to other particles. Each particle slips around others according to local forces acting on it [7]. The relationship between the particles is not arbitrary, nor is it statically pre-determined.

A third principle is *redundancy*. In Modern thought, redundancy is inherently wasteful, the reverse of optimization. Modern design optimizes each part or sub-system of a building to perform a single, pre-determined task. Once designed for this task, it is serially repeated throughout. For instance, a structural bay only provides structural stability, and it consists of as few types of columns and beams as possible. Cladding, on the other hand, provides only weather-tight enclosure. Cladding should be accomplished with the fewest panel sizes. Ideally, one panel would be repeated throughout. Structure should not contribute to weather-tight enclosure, which is not its task. Likewise, cladding should be non-structural. This conception of optimization is so entrenched that many designers consider it self-evidently true, yet the result is fragile architecture. Because the cladding is non-structural, any failure of the structure destroys the cladding as well. Because the structure is non-cladding, its contribution to shelter is negated and one crack of a cladding panel breaches the envelope. Buildings have few, if any, backup systems (i.e., redundancies) that allow them to resist the erosive forces of Nature [8].

Optimization by assigning parts an isolated task and then repeating the same parts everywhere is not the only way. In fact, this does not lead to optimal results in many cases. Optimization by means of redundancy and variation is the way of Nature, and the new movement is beginning to explore this alternative.

The new conception of system is connected to the study of natural systems, and particularly biological systems. This perspective is referred to by various names, including biomorphic, morphogenetic and biomimetic architecture. The principles of differentiation, consistency and redundancy are drawn from the observation of biological systems. The effort to transfer the behavior of these systems into architecture blurs the distinction between the natural and the manufactured.

> A systemic change is on the horizon, whereby the boundary between the "natural" and the "manufactured" will no longer exist. The complex interaction between form, material and structure of natural material systems has informed new "biomimetic" industrial processes, generating new high-performance materials. New processes are having a compelling impact on many industries, and new materials are radically transforming aerospace and maritime design and medicine. [...] Biomimetic strategies that integrate form, material and structure into a single process are being adopted from the nanoscale right up to the design and construction of very large buildings [9].

Interest in biological systems is connected to bottom-up thinking and materials research. Here, a key concept is *corporeality*.

The concept of corporeality is often used interchangeably with materiality, but there is an important distinction. Corporeality refers to material that is of or related to a body, consisting of flesh and bone, or something like flesh and bone. The concept includes a metaphorical aspect, which has roots in the doctrine of the Eucharist (*corporalis*), in which bread becomes or represents the body of Christ. Corporeality has an anatomical connotation, referring to material subdivided into systems of interrelated parts, which though distinct, work together to produce a larger action or effect, as in a living body. Architecture can be thought of as corporeal matter because it too is segmented and heterogeneous while unified in function. Corporeal thinking acknowledges the need for a distinction and specialization of architectural parts, as well as a mutual effect. It observes and responds to the tension between parts, seeking to make them at once articulated and integrated. Corporeal thinking therefore involves an interest in tectonics. Just as corporeality defines a sub-class of materiality, corporeal thinking describes a special approach to tectonics. Corporeal thinkers see the joint as a generative force affecting the whole. Since the type and articulation of joints depends on the materials used, joints provide a vehicle through which the properties of materials shape the whole [10].

Designers who follow the Modern tradition often condemn proponents of complex architecture for arbitrary form-making, assuming that the highly-articulated results are decorative, but proponents of the new movement do not generally pursue form for form's sake. On the contrary, complex architecture comes from a deep analysis of biological systems. It seeks a way of organizing space and material based on the resilience and beauty of living things. Its closest historical cousin might be Art Nouveau. Art Nouveau captured some of the complexity and dynamism of biological systems, but it did so with visually stylized floral and animal motifs. The new approach, in contrast, abstracts away from the literal appearance of living things, and instead follows underlying organizational patterns, often at the molecular or genetic scales, which are captured in the principles of differentiation, consistency, redundancy and corporeality. In this regard, complex architecture might more precisely be called genetic architecture.

Feedback Loop

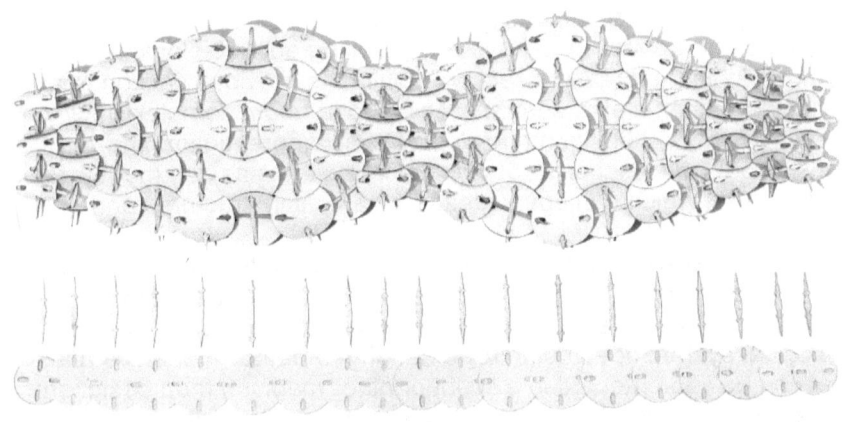

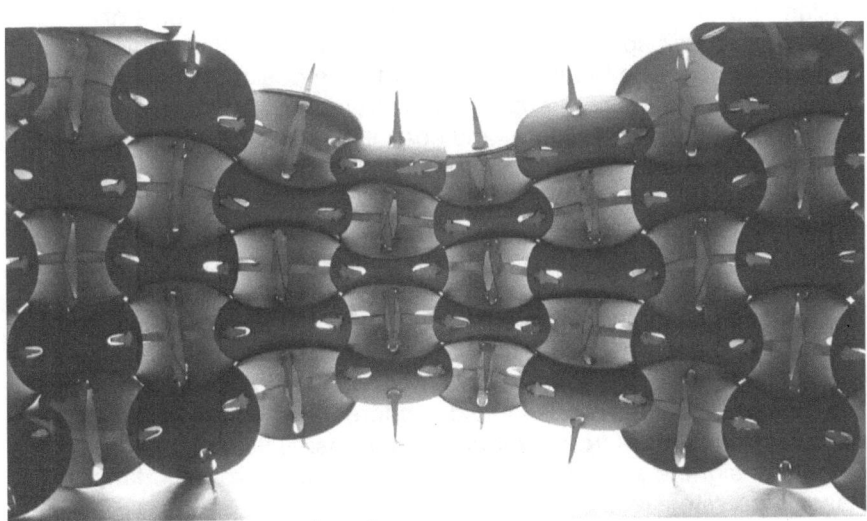

31 Cladding study, museum board

Biological and Man-made Systems

BIOLOGICAL SYSTEMS AND INSPIRATION

Biological systems can spark creative insight. Their study provides a flow of stimulating information to designers' imagination, helping them see beyond their previous experiences, showing them new ways to shape habitable structures. The diversity of structures found in nature is immense, providing new models to explore, test, hybridize and transform. This way of thinking about biological systems complements the previous section. While the previous section treats biological systems as a source of knowledge about complexity, which reveals high-level design principles such as differentiation and consistency, this section treats biological systems as rich models for architecture, which can spark ideas for particular structures and spaces.

When seeking inspiration in a biological system, what characteristics of the system are relevant? It is the rules and interactions that drive the organizing pattern of the system. If a biological system does not imply a set of geometric, interactive rules that can be implemented in a script or other medium, then designers have little chance of harnessing its complexity. Through an examination of images, samples or specimens, designers need to distill, at least to some extent, the simple building blocks that drive the system, so they can reproduce it, reinterpret it, and manipulate it in design. Furthermore, if designers examine images, samples or specimens and it sparks no architectural ideas, then this particular system might not be fertile. It should catalyze designers' imagination, enabling them to imagine architectural structures and spaces. While biology is inherently structural and spatial, these aspects are not always clear in a particular system.

When studying biology, designers sometime ask whether they should respect the form-function relationships in a system. For example, when studying the tunnels produced by ants, should designers extract the pattern of tunnels and the rules of their generation, leaving behind the arrangement of specific uses such as food storage and egg incubation, or should the function of the tunnels remain tethered to the form as designers reinterpret it? When studying the stalks of palm leaves, should designers use the idea of bundled, fibrous strands apart from their power to transmit fluids to the leaf? Should designers study the form of a system apart from the function associated with it?

Understanding the function of an organism is not required. In fact, tying form to function can hamper creativity. If a plant develops broad surfaces (i.e., leaves) to maximize sun exposure, then it would be too restrictive to create broad surfaces in a building only to maximize sun exposure. Designers can reinterpret such a feature to do many things, from providing structure to shedding water to framing views to ventilating. It is not necessary even to know what an organism is (plant, animal, bacterium), much less how it functions, in order to gain insight.

This disregard for function does not indicate a formalistic bias, but rather, a deliberate escape from functionalistic bias. Functionalism holds that the form of a building is properly derived from a program of human activities. Functionalists often extend this idea to Nature, accepting a teleological view of biology. In this view, organisms acquire forms in order to enact life-enhancing functions. A lion has sharp claws to grab and kill antelopes. An owl has large eyes to see rodents at night. A cardinal has colored feathers to attract a mate. The form of an organism does not emerge to serve a pre-established function. To the contrary, form emerges from a process of genetic mutation. Once a form exists, it either provides survival value or not, depending on environmental factors such as availability of food and exposure to predators. The functionality of an organism works itself out after its form erupts.

The inspiration-driven study of biological systems follows Nature's lead. It starts with form, structure, pattern or tectonic, extracted from Nature and reinterpreted for architecture, and then seeks to interface it with a context to find unexpected applications.

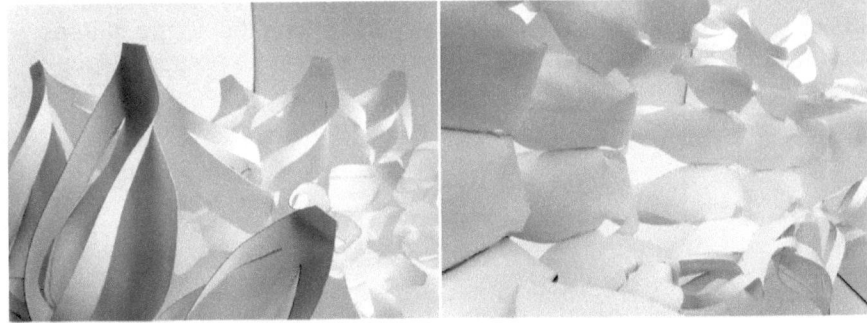

32 Structural study, paper

DYNAMIC AND STATIC

Complex things are interactive and responsive, and this leads experimental designers to an interest in dynamism rather than stasis. *Dynamism* is the study and pursuit of change rather than stability, movement rather than fixedness. Since architecture is a predominately stationary thing, it becomes dynamic in a manner different from a river or an automobile, which moves aggressively. Architecture embodies change through variety in its parts, rather than through movement. As inhabitants move through a varied building, they experience a discontinuous background.

Consider the ways we experience change in Nature. The direct way is to encounter moving elements such as wind or sun, but we can also experience change indirectly by observing the diversity of organisms, which result from a process of evolution. As we walk through a forest, we experience many trees, each the same type of thing, but simultaneously possessing myriad differences. The trees are the same in kind, but different in degree, that is, varied in measurements and intensity of qualities within a consistent formal structure.

Architecture can embody change in the indirect manner, but it does not have to do so. Much architecture from the 14th and 20th centuries sought stasis by minimizing variety in structural elements, spatial modules, and material qualities. It emphasized repetition, symmetry and continuity. In contrast, the new movement seeks generally to embody differences in degree among parts of the same kind, in order to accentuate variety across the interrelated parts of a whole. This indirectly reveals the rich network of interactions between the parts, and between the parts and outside influences (e.g., program and site) that are part of a complex, changing world. A complex building seeks to be like a forest, not by mimicking the shape of trees, but by embodying the dynamic process that led to its present, static form.

Feedback Loop

INTEGRATION OF MATERIAL AND GEOMETRY

Early in the book we considered the emergent properties of materials as a source of inspiration and insight. In the sections just traversed, we found the digital equivalent: the emergent properties of geometry-generating scripts. In one case, the behavior of material fuels creativity; in the other, the behavior of geometry fuels it. Materials and geometry provide parallel starting points into and routes through the feedback loop. The adventure of experimental design can unfold along either route, yet the possibilities become richer still when the routes interweave.

By engaging both prototyping and scripting, designers amplify the potential for emergence, yet at the same time they intensify the challenge of resolving the tension between material and geometry. Experimental designers question the traditional approach, which gives priority to geometry. In this approach, an over-arching formal idea guides and constrains material choices.

> The most important distinction in our changing notions of architectural design is the shift from geometry as an abstract regulator of the materials of construction to a notion that matter and material behavior must be implicated in geometry itself. In the older models, the sovereign role of geometry was to regulate or impress itself upon the irrational and accidental condition of matter, thus measurement, proportion, and all of the elements of pure extension maintain a priority over that which they regulate [11].

In contrast to this approach, the new movement seeks an integration of material and geometry, in which key behaviors of a material are embedded in the behavior of a geometric structure (through the definition of its parameters) and in which geometry is used in a digitally-augmented fabrication process to push the limits of what materials can do. Each force, material and geometrical, influences the other.

INTEGRATION OF DESIGN AND CONSTRUCTION

Experimental designers embrace the digitally-augmented construction methods first developed in the aeronautical and automobile industries. These computer numeric controlled (cnc) manufacturing techniques augment and require an integration of design and construction. As these methods become popular in the production of buildings, more designers question conventional practice. Built on the principles of the early Industrial Revolution, the conventional approach segregates design and construction into sequential activities. First we design it, and then we build it. This approach is inefficient and error-prone.

New manufacturing techniques are not only changing long-standing models of business and collaboration, they are changing the way designers conceive and develop projects. Because digital output feeds directly to fabrication machinery, designers enjoy an empirical link to and influence over the act of full-scale making that has been largely denied to them since the onset of industrialization. Digitally-augmented fabrication bridges the gap between design and construction and grants unprecedented influence to designers over the realization of their ideas.

With this new power comes new responsibility. In order to take advantage of digital manufacturing, designers must first understand its capabilities and how these influence project conception and development. Just as a prototype or script possesses inherent limitations and latent possibilities, so also does a manufacturing process. The experimental application of a manufacturing process relies on designers' ability to probe its latent behaviors and direct its emergent outcomes toward innovative designs. Digital fabrication is the third medium of experimental architecture. As with prototypes and scripts, digital fabrication techniques are a source of inspiration. When designers engage all three, weaving them into a multifaceted feedback loop, emergence looms large.

ECONOMY

Mainstream designers often resist complex architecture on the grounds of expense. This is another example of the cultural bias against complexity. Complex things are not inherently more expensive or difficult to construct than simple things. Complexity merely requires a different kind of production process. After a century of Modernism, manufacturing infrastructure is geared toward fixed, repetitive units. Complex architecture, in contrast, requires mass-customization with digitally-augmented fabrication techniques. Support for mass-customization is spreading, but the infrastructure is still small by comparison. As it grows, the cost of mass-customization will continue to fall.

On a wider note, it is important to acknowledge that the assessment of economy is a value-judgment. What makes something economical is not just how much it costs, with the assumption that the lowest possible price is preferable. Instead, "economical" is an assessment of whether a product is worth what you paid. For example, people often buy toasters that cost *more* than the lowest-cost option. Why would they do this? Why pay $35 for a toaster, when sitting right next to it on a store's shelf is one for $15? Those who buy the $35 toaster, like those who buy the $15 version, are generally intelligent people seeking value for their money. Those who pay more recognize that a balance exists between what one pays and what one gets, and they look for the best balance rather than the lowest absolute price. Paying $15 for a shoddy toaster is not necessarily better than paying $35 for a toaster that looks good, functions well and lasts long. Many consumers evaluate the $35 toaster as more economical.

If complex architecture gives us more value than simple architecture, then people should be willing to pay more for it. This kind of thinking is alien to designers who reduce cost to a minimum without regard for value. They have adopted the market strategy of the shoddy toaster company, whose all-encompassing objective is minimum price.

Experimental designers, who often seek more complex products, are driven by a different strategy. They seek to add value rather than reduce cost. They are not minimalists who offer a bear-minimum product. They offer a product that seeks to enrich people's lives. Of course, this strategy requires them to demonstrate the value of their product, to convince customers that it is worthwhile to pay more. If designers want complex architecture, they should be prepared to convince customers that it is worth the price.

When facing this imperative, designers risk a relapse into functionalistic thinking. They might be tempted to argue the value of complex architecture in terms of programmatic or structural efficiency, or perhaps lower carbon footprints, but its value cannot be established on quantitative grounds. Instead, its value lies in the qualitative, in what it shows us about the world. Complex architecture intensifies awareness of the world's open-ended potential for change; it reveals the inner workings of living organisms; it confronts our senses with concentrated and nuanced stimulation; it is the antidote for those who feel drained by simplicity, sameness and sterility. Complex architecture confronts the lie of simplicity by showing the world as it really is: rich, teeming, growing, intricate, and filled with a wealth of prospects. Complex architecture is a reflection of a certain view of life, and it fuels that kind of life by embodying its qualities in the places where we dwell.

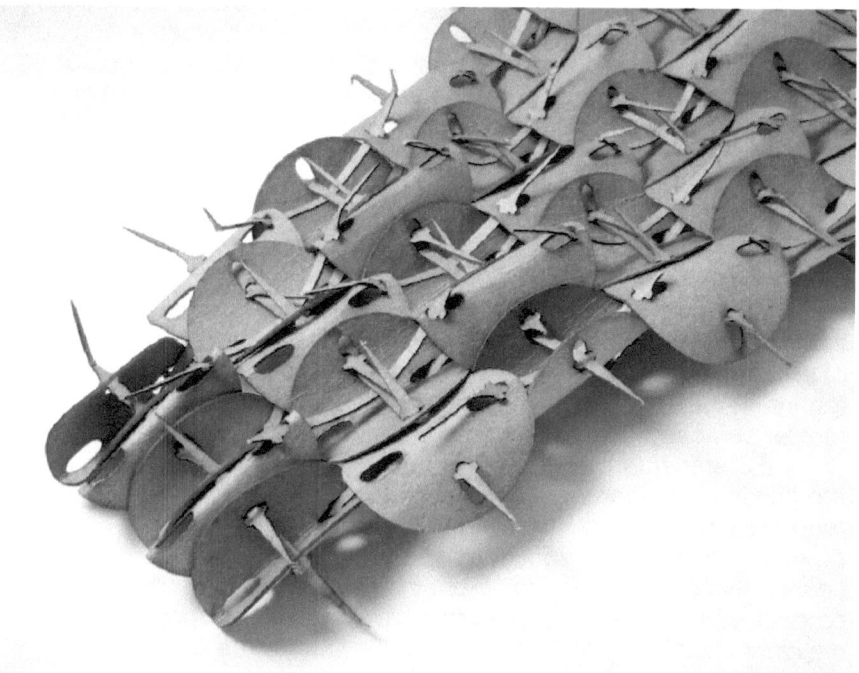

33 Cladding study, chipboard

Feedback Loop

COMPLEXITY AND ARTICULATION

The power of digitally-augmented manufacturing is the construction of complexity through mass-customization. Whereas traditional manufacturing produces uniformity, digital manufacturing produces ubiquitous difference. The key to this power is computer numeric control (cnc), which does not merely automate fabrication, but automates a system of parametric variation. In this regard, cnc fabrication is to manufacturing what generative scripting is to digital model-building. Parametric control is the engine of both.

As we saw in the previous section, some designers complain that digital fabrication is too expensive, but the advance of these techniques is not fundamentally a matter of money. The purpose of digital fabrication is not to save money; it is to express a different view of the world. Digital manufacturing offers a means to overcome Modern uniformity with complexity, and perhaps the most widespread manifestation of complexity is the articulated surface. While the smooth curved surface is capable of only a few variations (e.g., eggs and blobs), the articulated surface opens nearly boundless creative territory for cladding and structure. Rather than pursue the articulated surface as a form of applied decoration, complex architecture pursues it as a feature of an interactive system. Just as articulation of a living organism heightens at points of contact with the world: fingertip, eyelid, ear canal, teeth, the articulation of architecture heightens at its points of contact: at its enveloping skin. Rather than mute the interactive boundary between inside and out, it is accentuated.

Architecture is inherently complex since it is constructed by aggregating many discrete parts, components or members into a larger whole. Any desire for uniformity or smoothness cannot overcome the fact that architecture must be sub-divided, panelized and segmented. The new movement and its associated manufacturing techniques are more true to the nature of architecture, channeling and manipulating its inherent complexity, rather than pushing a false uniformity or smoothness.

THE FUTURE OF COMPLEX ARCHITECTURE

Despite its infancy, the new movement has already brought architecture to the cusp of a new aesthetic age. It is an age rediscovering the beauty of Nature and of materials. It is an age of technological progress and customization, in which material and digital meld. It is an age that rewards creativity and conviction. It is an age that recognizes the microscopic forces that order and drive the perceivable world. It seeks to organize this teeming world of atoms and genes according to human intentions, integrating natural order and human order. This genetic age promises to become the next great age of architecture. If it survives its infancy, it will drive the next long-term trend, not a passing fashion, but a new era dedicated to the expression of a new view of the world.

This future is not inevitable. The new movement could atrophy, leaving a void to be filled by other ideas. If this happens, the cause will come from within the movement itself. Some of its advocates embrace relativism and technological determinism, two ideas that could spell doom for the movement.

Relativists are wary of the very idea of a movement or of a cohesive aesthetic era. They prefer to keep their convictions "flexible" and not fight too hard for any particular idea. They fear the institutionalization of another static orthodoxy, which, once established, might strangle creative freedom. Their concerns seem warranted, since some past eras suffered this fate. Early 20th century thinkers embraced the view of mankind as a socially-determined animal, and the destructive effects of social engineering rippled through many disciplines, including architecture.

Technological determinists make the opposite error. They believe in the movement's inevitable success, and thus, they see no reason to defend it. They feel the irresistible pull of new technology, and they become preoccupied with the instrumentalization of designs. Recent literature is saturated with accounts of how a project was modeled, analyzed, documented and fabricated using new technology. Projects are explained predominately, if not exclusively, in terms of the tools used to produce them.

The relativist and the determinist seem different on the surface: one is tentative and the other is zealous, but these attitudes grow from a common cause: *disinterest in the ideas behind the new movement*. The relativist resists these ideas on the grounds that any idea held too firmly is dangerous, while the determinist resists on the grounds that ideas are powerless against the blind momentum of technological culture. Yet it is only the underlying ideas of complex architecture that can clarify the new movement's identity, explain its methods, justify its goals and prepare the way for long-term influence.

As this brief introduction indicates, complex architecture has a solid ideological foundation, which is its true engine and compass. Furthermore, its root ideas are integrated with a distinctive and powerful methodology, which in turn integrates with a collection of distinctive and powerful technologies. The new movement is developing an integrated system of design with implications for both process and product. This system, in contrast to those conceived in prior ages, is inherently open, evolutionary, and responsive. Far from saddling designers with another constricting orthodoxy, the new movement champions creativity and its preconditions.

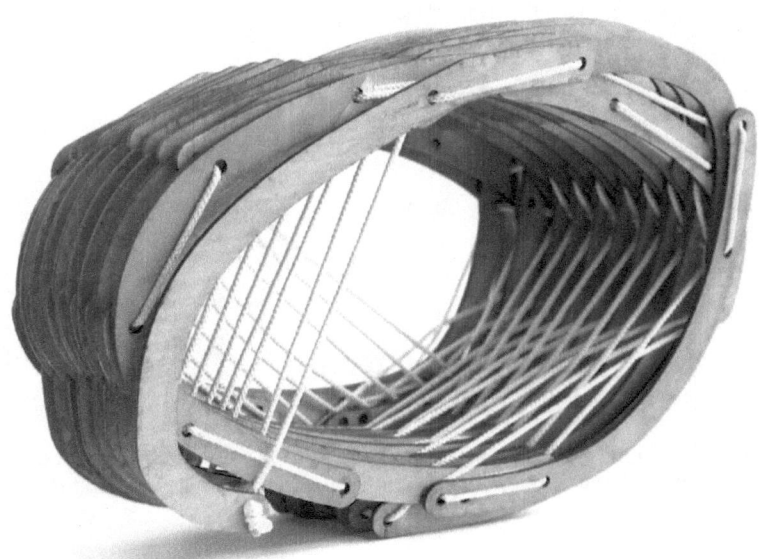

34 Tectonic study, wood and rope

IMAGE CREDITS

Cover incorporates image of material study in aluminum by Kelly Fox.

1   p. 6, Nathan Currier-Groh
2   p. 14, Paul Mattek
3   p. 16, Justin White
4   p. 18, Cassie Hibbert
5   p. 19, Nick Reiter
6   p. 21, Jeff Welch
7   p. 24, Justin White
8   p. 25, Kyle Talbott
9   p. 26, Kyle Talbott
10   p. 27, Jeff Welch
11   p. 27, Nathan Currier-Groh
12   p. 31, Jeff Welch
13   p. 31, Christine Krueger
14   p. 32, Jeff Welch
15   p. 34, Justin White
16   p. 36, Jasenko Badic
17   p. 39, Nathan Currier-Groh
18   p. 44, Erik Walsh
19   p. 45, Tuan Tran
20   p. 48, Ryan O'Connor
21   p. 50, David Gleisner
22   p. 51, Ian Kearns
23   p. 52, Cassie Hibbert
24   p. 53, Kyle Talbott
25   p. 54, Cassie Hibbert
26   p. 57, Kyle Talbott
27   p. 57, Nathan Currier-Groh
28   p. 59, Ted Kimble
29   p. 61, Ted Kimble
30   p. 63, Ian Kearns
31   p. 67, Nathan Currier-Groh
32   p. 69, Christine Krueger
33   p. 74, Nathan Currier-Groh
34   p. 77, Jessie Wilcox

Work shown in images was produced in design studios conducted by the author at the University of Wisconsin-Milwaukee School of Architecture and Urban Planning.

NOTES

1   For an introduction to the role of a view of the world in art and architecture see *The Romantic Manifesto*, Ayn Rand, Penguin Books, New York, 1975.

2   For an introduction to the history of Complexity Science see *Chaos: Making a New Science*, James Gleick, Penguin Books, New York, 1987.

3   For more information about the connection between bottom-up thinking and robotics see *How the Body Shapes the Way We Think: A New View of Intelligence*, Rolf Pfeifer and Josh Bongard, MIT Press, Cambridge, 2007.

4   Stephen Wolfram, "How Do Simple Programs Behave?", *AD: Programming Cultures*, 76:4(2006).

5   *How the Body Shapes the Way We Think: A New View of Intelligence*, Rolf Pfeifer and Josh Bongard, MIT Press, Cambridge, 2007, p. 85.

6   For more information on the relationship between intentions and exploration see *Plans and Situated Actions: The Problem of Human Machine Communication*, Lucy A. Suchman, Cambridge University Press, Cambridge, 1987.

7   The cake mix analogy is taken from Pia Ednie-Brown, "All-Over, Over-All: Biothing and Emergent Composition," *AD: Programming Cultures,* 76:4(2006).

8   Michael Weinstock, "Self-Organization and the Structural Dynamics of Plants," *AD: Techniques in Morphogenetic Design*, 76:2(2006).

9   Ibid.

10   Kyle Talbott, "3D Print as Corporeal Design Medium," *International Journal of Architectural Computing*, 4:4(2006).

11   *Atlas of Novel Tectonics*, Reiser + Umemoto, Princeton Architectural Press, New York, 2006, p. 72.

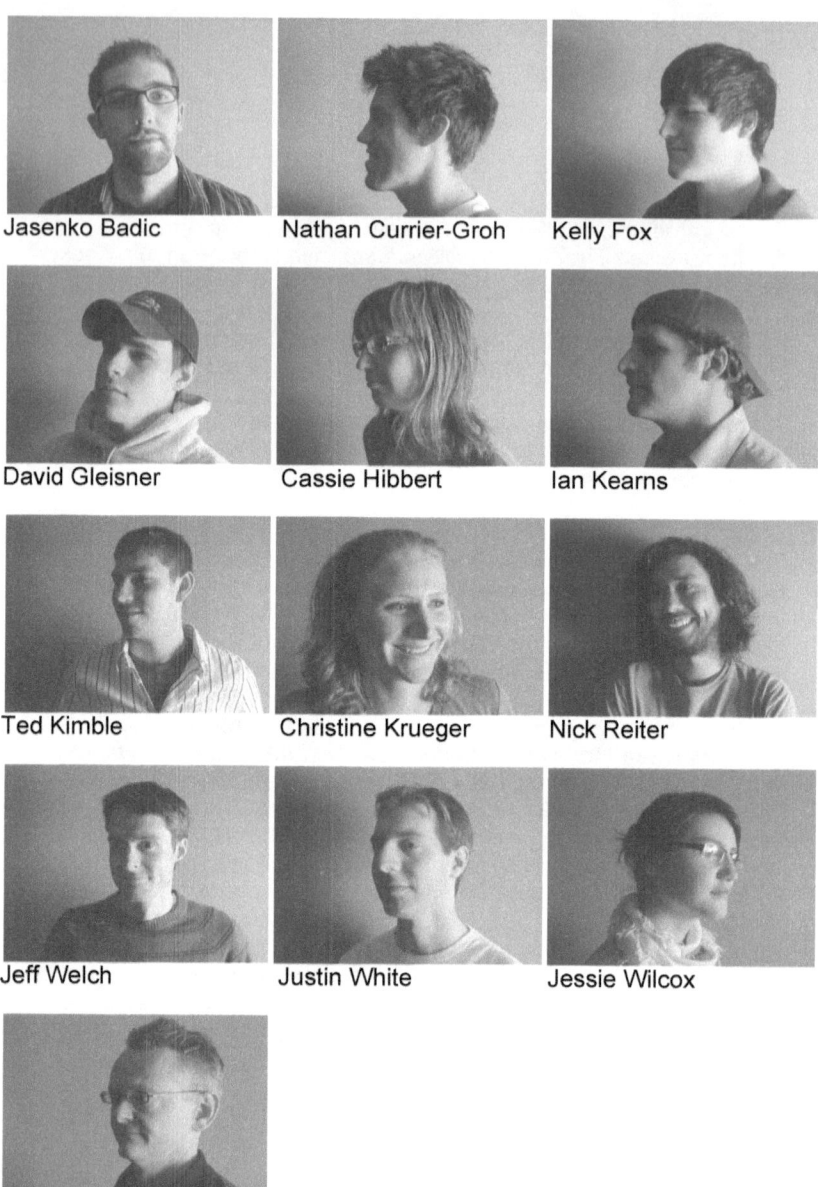

Jasenko Badic   Nathan Currier-Groh   Kelly Fox

David Gleisner   Cassie Hibbert   Ian Kearns

Ted Kimble   Christine Krueger   Nick Reiter

Jeff Welch   Justin White   Jessie Wilcox

Kyle Talbott is an Associate Professor of Architecture at the University of Wisconsin in Milwaukee, USA, where he lives with his loving wife MeLain and conducts design-based research, academic studios and reflective practice with an emphasis on theory and application of emerging digital technology and experimental use of low-tech building materials.

Feedback Loop